A Conspiracy to Create Joy

Circus Spirituality
Beyond the Center Ring

By

Catherine Martin, Ph.D.

Published by Linus Publications, Inc.
Deer Park, NY 11729

Copyright © 2011 by Linus Publications
All Rights Reserved.

ISBN 13: 978-1-60797-239-6
ISBN 10: 1-60797-239-5

No part of this publication may be reproduced, stored in a retrieval system, or transmitted, in any form or by any means, electronic, mechanical, photocopying, recording, or otherwise, without the prior permission of the publisher.

Printed in the United States of America.

Print Numbers   5   4   3   2   1

To Bob, whose love makes the journey ever joyful

and

To the Circus Nuns who conspire to create joy wherever their nomadic lives take them

Forever friends - Sister Dorothy Fabritze, MSC and Sister Bernard Overkamp, MSC

New friends – Little Sisters of Jesus, Little Sister Jo and Little Sister Priscilla

ACKNOWLEDGEMENTS

In addition to my husband Bob and the circus nuns, Sisters Dorothy, Bernard, Jo and Priscilla, there are many people who were supportive in the process of bringing this manuscript to publication. I will never be able to acknowledge all of them but it is important for me to mention at least some of those who have made this work possible.

My first note of gratitude goes to all of the circus people who gave so generously of their time for interviews or to complete the research survey in the midst of very demanding schedules. Thank you also to those who made me welcome at the various circuses I visited, spending time with me in every day conversations and sharing the simple joys of circus life as well as the results of their hard labor, the grandeur of the performances I witnessed.

Fr. Jerry Hogan and all of those who minister to the circus people have my deepest admiration. I am grateful to the lay people, priests, and sisters who are part of the Circus and Traveling Show Ministries. They have my sincere appreciation for inviting me to be part of the Annual Conference in Sarasota, Florida and for sharing their stories with me with such openness and joy. They are all a true inspiration.

My home base, the College of St. Elizabeth continues to be a source of encouragement for my work, especially the outstanding faculty members of the Philosophy and Theology program. A special word of appreciation goes to Sr. Diane Collesano, SC, who reviewed the manuscript and offered many helpful suggestions. The CSE Institutional Review Board approved my project but also expressed an enthusiasm that helped me to keep moving forward. Colleagues in Psychology invited a group of circus people to come and share about their life and spirituality with members of the campus community. The Center for Theological and Spiritual Development at the college offered me the opportunity to share my research in progress at its annual Spirituality Convocation. To all of those involved in making these events possible and to my students, those in ministry programs, deacon candidates, graduate and undergraduate theology students, I say thank you for deepening the level of discussion on the world of circus spirituality.

I also offer my thanks to those who translated my questionnaire and the responses of non-English speaking circus folks into Spanish and Portuguese, Sister Elsa Jeronimo, CSJB, Jessica Hadley and Veronica Mazzini.

Thank you also to all of my family and friends who have waited to see this project come to completion and who form the network of love which make it possible for me to be who I am and pursue my dreams and visions.

Finally, thank you to all those who read this work, extend its meaning in your conversations, and give it life by your own contribution to the conspiracy to create joy in our world.

Table of Contents

Dedication iii
Acknowledgements v
Introduction ix

CHAPTER 1
Circus Life 1

CHAPTER 2
Where the Community Gathers is Sacred Space 13

CHAPTER 3
God Is on the Journey Not Only at the Destination 31

CHAPTER 4
Identity Is Not Captured by a Task or Title 49

CHAPTER 5
Interdependence Is Grace and Responsibility 59

CHAPTER 6
Ministry Makes a Difference 87

CHAPTER 7
Performance Is Meant to Be a Gift of Love 113

CHAPTER 8
Concluding Remarks 127

Introduction

"I long to dwell in your tent forever and take refuge in the shelter of your wings." (Psalm 61:4 NIV)

Some stories deserve to be told. I have been fortunate enough to hear one of those narratives first hand from those who live it day in and day out. It is a simple story of living in response to God's grace, in awareness of God's presence. It is about an inner spirit hidden within people who live an otherwise very public life. It is the report of beautiful blessings behind the scenes at the circus, backstage in that mysterious world caravanned from town to town by a nomadic company of passing strangers. During their brief visits, the travelers live at the edges of the comfortable reality known to the locals. There on the fringes, the circus spirit which lightens minds and hearts, releasing unburdened childhood joy in others is secretly being nourished by familiar trust in God and carefully cultivated care for one another.

In the parable told by their lives, those who follow the circus route simultaneously undertake both a physical and a spiritual journey. Their discipline and simple lifestyle undergirds the powerful grace, the extravagant beauty, and abundance of joy they offer to audiences at each stop along the road.

The parallels between non-circus life and circus life are numerous enough to have inspired a variety of common expressions. We hear people say, "My life is a circus." Facing situations where many different things are happening at the same time, phrases such as, "What a circus." or "I'm juggling too many things right now." easily come to mind. Attempting difficult tasks can inspire the comment, "I'm working without a net here." Bil Keane's delightful long-lasting comic strip about the humorous side of life with young children is aptly titled "The Family Circus."

Circus images are evoked when many demanding activities occur simultaneously, where apparently untamable situations are being faced, and where a bit of humor pervades the whole hectic reality. The circus gives the impression of an order that is always verging on chaos or catastrophe. It takes you to the edge and then, as your breath alternates between gasps of fear and sighs of relief, it all ends safely and happily.

As hectic as the performance is, so too is the life behind the scenes of the circus. The two constant rhythms around which existence is orchestrated are performance schedules and travel times.

Do you ever feel like your life is a three-ring circus with many activities claiming your attention at once? Are you called upon to perform in important roles for other people on a regular basis? Do you spend a great deal of time driving yourself and others from place to place? Reading these pages may help you to discover some ways real life circus folks integrate spirituality into their lives of constant movement and commitment to excellence in performing for others.

How do circus people who are constantly on the move, living in close quarters, and working at high pressure jobs in the public eye, maintain a spiritual dimension to their lives? What is the relationship of their way of life to a consciousness of the divine?

These questions flow from my interactions with many circus people who remain close to God in an environment that is antithetical to the classic prescription for spiritual development, i.e., taking time to settle down in silent solitude. Those who study the spiritual arts and those who live hectic lives may both find new wisdom in exploring this unique migrant community.

God wants to break through to all people. For those in the circus, the challenges of their lifestyle can create openness to an aspect of reality which transcends their physical experience. Acutely aware of the fragile nature of security, they are motivated to trust in something/someone greater than themselves to sustain them.

People on the move are frequently conscious of the depths of a sacred underlying landscape which gives the lie to an apparent disconnection of places and tyranny of time. Although the stresses of danger, work pressure, and constant movement to new locations can threaten spiritual sensibilities, many in the circus are able to transform those limitations into sources of spiritual strength.

Introduction xi

My project here is to demonstrate the spiritual vitality of people in the circus world, to outline dimensions of their lives which contribute to the shape of their spiritual expressions, to demonstrate the value of mutual ministry, and to provide some insights which can be transferred to life outside the circus arena.

The spiritual lives and practices of migrant workers in general and certain subgroups of migrants, such as migrant farm workers have been researched in recent years.[1] The same has not been done for that group of performance workers who follow the circuit of a traveling show.[2] Because they move as a unit when they are part of a particular circus and do not travel to find work, circus people are not usually studied within the context of the migrant worker.

In these pages I will reflect specifically on the spirituality of those who live and work on the road in the circus world. Where appropriate, the literature on migrant spirituality in general will be related to the specific setting of migrant spirituality in circus life.

Several authors have produced inspiring books using circus performances as metaphors for powerful spiritual realities. Thomas Merton's close friend, poet Robert Lax had a love affair with the circus which he expressed in such critically acclaimed works as "Circus of the Sun,"[3] in which he exclaims, "The circus is a song of praise, a song of praise unto the Lord."[4] Throughout this work Lax relates the movements of the sun with the movement of the circus and uses both to evoke Wisdom's creative activity since the dawn of time, the process of creating all in love.

---

1. Some essays relating to migrant farm worker spirituality include: Ana Maria Peneda. "Imagenes de Dios en el camino: retablos, ex-votos, milagritos, and murals," *Theological Studies*. (Washington: Jun 2004.) Vol. 65, Iss. 2,. 364.; Olivia Ruiz. "Border of Death, Valley of Life: An Immigrant Journey of Heart and Spirit," *The International Migration Review*. (New York: Fall 2003.) Vol. 37, Iss. 3, 903.; Maria Frascati Lochhead. "Being at the edge: Retracing the spiritual journey of the migrant to God and self," *Migration World Magazine*. (Staten Island: 1999.) Vol. 27, Iss. 4, 18
2. Tino Wallenda's memoir is an exception: *Walking the Straight and Narrow: Lessons in Faith from the High Wire*. 2005. Works about circus life in general are more numerous, see: Victoria B. Cristiani Rossi. *Spangles, Elephants, Violets and Me: The Circus Inside Out*, 2007; Dorothy Herbert. Dorothy Herbert, Riding Sensation of the Age: A Memoir, 2005.
3. His association with the renowned performing circus family, the Cristianis, with whom he traveled through western Canada in 1950, provided the source for most of his reflections. He also traveled in Italy for a brief time with another circus, The Alfred North Zoo Circus, in the company of one of the workers rather than with the performers. The book *Circus Days and Nights* includes all of Lax's poem cycles on circus life.
4. Robert Lax. *Circus Days and Nights* (Woodstock, NY: The Overlook Press, 2000) 36.

Circus performance as metaphor for spirituality is a familiar theme in Henri Nouwen's writings. His fascination with the circus comes through in *Clowning in Rome,* where he explores the role of the clown in helping us realize we are not alone in our weakness. The role of the clown is analogous to that of the minister of grace.

Another of his published treatments of the circus world is an accounting of his sojourn with the Flying Rodleighs, trapeze artists of a European circus troupe. His reflections were published as "Circus Diary: Parts I and II" in the *New Oxford Review*.[5]

Nouwen proposes that God is the catcher in our spiritual lives, the one in whom we must have total trust if we are to execute our performance with success. He extended that concept to include God as the ultimate catcher for those facing death. "Dying is trusting in the catcher....Just stretch out your arms and hands and trust, trust, trust."[6]

Sam Keen took up this same topic. At sixty-one years of age he took a trapeze training course. His experience and reflections resulted in his book *Learning to Fly: Trapeze-Reflections on Fear, Trust, and the Joy of Letting Go.* As the title indicates, the analogies he has drawn are very similar to those of Henri Nouwen.

The ritual inevitably connected with circus life and performance has been titled "Liturgy of the People" by Abbe Maurice Zundel. The romance of the setting up and taking down of the tent, the grace and courage which combine in the work of the trapeze artists, the clown who touches hearts through weakness, and many other aspects of the circus provide rich images which point to deep spiritual mysteries.

I am neither the inspiring poet Robert Lax, nor the gifted spiritual guide Henri Nouwen but I do have a story to tell. It is about life in the circus. While we know some of the analogies of circus life from Nouwen and Lax and also Sam Keen and Maurice Zundel, the spiritual life of the actual circus performer has not been shared. No-

---

5 Nouwen spent several weeks traveling with the Flying Rodleighs trapeze troupe in the Circus Barum. See "Circus Diary – Part I" and "Circus Diary – Part II" in *New Oxford Review,* (June 1993 and July-August 1993.)

6 Henri Nouwen, quoted in his Epilogue by Michael Ford *Wounded Prophet: A Portrait of Henri J. M. Nouwen,* (Image, 2002).

Introduction   xiii

one has studied that unique group of migrant workers who make up the circus world. Those topics are closer to the primary goal here. I want to talk less about spiritual metaphors and more about the real people who live the hectic reality of life in the circus.

The performance is not the whole of the circus life, and the acts done for the audiences are not the only actions of the people who provide those moments of wonder which activate the emotions. While the performance cannot be separated from any discussion of circus life, the material here will focus on the whole experience of living in a community gathered for the purpose of that performance. In that vein, a view of the everyday life of those who make the circus happen can give a different perspective on one's own Life as well.

In addition to my own observations and informal conversations over the past 10 years, my formal interviews and questionnaires document the responses of sixty-five circus people to questions about their life and spirituality.[7] They ranged in age from 18 to 83, roughly 1/3 male and 2/3 female, with circus life experience from 6 months to 67 years.[8]

This research has also included studying circus promotional material, personal journals, and a large collection of published newspaper and magazine articles, and four television segments on the topic of ministry in the circus aired by CNN, the BBC, and the Hallmark Channel about people in the circus. I have also read a number of memoirs and autobiographical works written by circus performers and have reviewed material on other migrants and their spirituality to assess its relevance to circus spirituality.

Although I am interested in looking at the data gathered for this study of circus spirituality, I am also convinced that a consideration of spiritual devotion and expression has elements that cannot be drawn from scientifically verifiable evidence alone. My close association with the very few women religious who

---

7   This research was approved by the College of St. Elizabeth Institutional Review Board. The English –language questionnaires were translated into Spanish and Portuguese and distributed to those who speak those languages as well.

8   The age range distribution is: 18-39 years – 41%; 40-59 years – 24%; 60-83 years – 35%. The years of experience distribution is: <1-9 years – 45%; 10-30 years -23%; 30-67 years – 32%.

minister in the circus community has provided invaluable insights into circus life and spirituality.[9]

I have stayed with two Missionaries of the Sacred Heart in the circus community for a week in New Mexico and a week in Baltimore, plus many days and nights visiting them in circuses in New Jersey, New York, Pennsylvania, Connecticut, and Washington, D.C. and have spoken with them on a weekly basis for the ten years in which they have been a part of the circus. I have also had long conversations and correspondence with two Little Sisters of Jesus who have dedicated their life to the circus community and have been generous in providing me with valuable information.

All of these women religious are full time circus employees and are thus ministers from within the community. They work with the support of the Subcommittee on the Pastoral Care of Migrants, Refugees, and Travelers within the United States Conference of Catholic Bishops' Secretariat of Cultural Diversity in the Church.[10]

Their leadership has allowed me to attend their annual Conference of Circus and Traveling Show Ministries to learn from those who work with migrant performers. This yearly gathering has been bringing the ministers together since 1992.[11] This includes circus people as well as carnival folk, rodeo riders, and race car drivers, all of whom order their lives around a series of performances scheduled in a wide variety of communities in any given season.

The intent of my study has not been to demonstrate how unique circus life is so that others feel distanced from people in the circus and then simply become amazed at or perhaps feel sorry for the difficult life they lead. On the contrary, it seems that seeing how

---

9 Currently there are two women religious living and working full time in the circus. They are Missionary Sisters of the Most Sacred Heart of Jesus. Two other women religious are Little Sisters of Jesus who have been in the circus for over 25 years. They are now working in the circus 'spot dates' (doing individual. shows throughout the year).
10 Father Alan Figueroa Deck, SJ, was the first Executive Director of this recently formed USCCB Secretariat. The Vatican counterpart for this ministry is housed within the Pontifical Council for the Pastoral Care of Migrants and Itinerant People. Their eighth International Congress of the Pastoral Care of Circus and Traveling Show People was held in Rome, December 2010.
11 The annual conference in Florida is scheduled during winter quarters when the mud circuses are on break and the other traveling shows have completed their annual circuit. On the last two days there are special Masses, one for all the circus people who have died during the last season, and one for all circus folks. These are traditionally celebrated at St. Martha's Church in Sarasota.

someone else in different but similarly challenging circumstances copes with that way of life can give others a new perspective on their own situation.

If one sees others living tremendously busy lives with many pressures and demands on their time and ability who still balance relationships with God, family, friends, and others, one might catch a glimpse of the possibilities for oneself in reflection. If one looks at those who in the midst of all they face are finding some ways to stay close to God and /or to become more spiritually whole persons, one may receive some fresh clues about one's own struggles.

I am writing to capture what I can of the experience of people who balance a very public life with an equally private life within their shared community. These are people who live in the circus and who witness to a closeness to God in that whirlwind of activity. I am writing to share this reality in a way that will affirm the circus community, motivate non-circus people in their own spiritual struggles, and note the difficulties and challenges to maintaining and developing spiritual sensitivities for those who live a migratory life. By sharing some insights into the spiritual lives of circus people, both performers and those backstage folks who make the performance possible, some principles may be revealed which those in other situations can adapt to their own spiritual circumstances.

In the process of looking at circus life, we will be seeing not a perfect group of people, but people who struggle with sin and evil, limited resources, injustices, and personal faults and failures. It is from this context, parallel to those in many other communities, that we can draw out the attitudes and practices with which members of the circus community address their particular circumstances. In that way we can highlight their approach to a relationship to God and a desire for harmony with all of reality permeated with God's presence.

The initial chapter will give an overview of circus life to familiarize readers with the relatively unknown terrain of the lives of those who are often only viewed from a grandstand perspective. The final chapter will summarize certain conclusions about circus spirituality and its implications for spirituality outside the circus world. The chapters in-between will describe areas which reveal some of texture of the spiritual lives of those in the circus community. Special attention will be given to conversations held with current members of various circus troupes in the United States to discern patterns of seeking the holy in the midst of close living quarters and repeated movement from place to place throughout the yearly performance cycle. Each chapter will look at one of the six spiritual principles I have identified as permeating circus life:

- Where the community gathers is Sacred Space.
- God is on the journey not only at the destination.
- Identity is not captured by a task or title.
- Interdependence is grace and responsibility.
- Ministry makes a difference.
- Performance is meant to be a gift of love.

Each topic of reflection will be reviewed from the perspective of the circus experience of this reality. Stories of some spiritual responses to that aspect of circus life will highlight each principle. Those approaches will be put in conversation with traditional wisdom of the spiritual life to discover common threads. Then a performance metaphor will move the discussion to a different level with the hope of encouraging readers to discover some support for their own spiritual life. One approach to reading might include asking how the spiritual principle being highlighted might connect to one's own life experience.

My focus will be on what Alex Garcia-Rivera calls the "little stories" of people's lives. It presumes an incarnational spirituality in which the divine is revealed in the ordinary. This coincides with the category of 'lo cotidiano' described by theologians Ana Maria Pineda, Ada Maria Isasi Diaz and Maria Pilar Aquino among others. This concept posits that everyday reality is the locus of connection with the sacred. We will look for God under the tent and in the back lots, in the proverbial smell of the greasepaint and in the roar of the crowds.

We begin now at the break of day, long before the performance, where circus folks rouse from their sleep to begin the work of transforming a vacant space into a world of wonder. In the early passages of his poem "Circus of the Sun," Robert Lax casts the raising of the circus tent in an empty field as a spiritual experience recapturing the first moments of creation when "the earth was formless and empty." In their daily toil, the circus folks echo and continue the creative work of God.

> We have seen all the days of creation in one day: this is the day of the waking dawn and all over the field the people are moving, they are coming to praise the Lord: and it is now the first day of creation….We were there in the beginning for we were there in the morning and we saw the rising of the tent and we have known how it was in the beginning. We have known the creation of the firmament: and of the water, and of the dry land, and of the creatures that moved in the deep, and of the creatures that moved on the land, and of the creation of men: the waking of acrobats. We have known these things from the beginning of the morning, for we woke early. We rose and came to the field.[12]

---

12   Robert Lax. *Circus Days and Nights*. (Woodstock, NY: Overlook Press, 2000) 35.

CHAPTER 1

Circus Life

"You must never build houses, sow seeds or plant vineyards… but must always live in tents. Then you will live a long time in the land where you are nomads." (Jeremiah 35:7 NIV)

When people say, "My life is like a circus," they are usually referring to lots of fast-paced activity with many different things happening at once. For those people who actually live in the circus, references to the exciting show which they present are only a small fraction of what real circus life is like. This chapter will provide a glimpse of life beyond the Big Top. It is meant to help the reader to understand what life is like behind the scenes in a traveling show.

The people who create the circus are very much like the people who come night after night to watch the results of their hard work. Circus folks have friends and family and very real feelings. In this section, I want to introduce you to a few aspects of the type of life lived by the people who make up the circus world and give you a bit of a snapshot of who they are. Then we will begin to look at how circus people connect with the spiritual dimensions of reality within their unique context.

As lively as a circus performance is, so too is the life behind the scenes of the circus. The two rhythms around which existence is orchestrated are performance schedules and travel times. There is very little down time in a circus,

Saturday and Sunday are prime entertainment times, as are most holidays, with even more performances than on weekdays. Non-performance days are days of load out, which means taking the tents and trappings down, travel to the next destination, and load in for the next show. In the words of a seventy-year old circus man, "You are on the road and you work from sun-up to sundown all seven days per week." The MSC Sisters' circus journal gives repeated accounts of visits by members of religious communities and other friends in which the conversations took place while the visitors pitched in to sell ride tickets, serve dinner, or help out in some other way. There is little time for relaxed catching up during the circus season, except in the brief time after the final show and before it is time to turn in for the evening.

Circuses, particularly the smaller shows, run on very tight profit margins. Performances are held as frequently as possible, as long as there is any hope of an audience. Triple packs, three shows in one day, are the norm on weekends.

Performers and workers join the owners in concern about the size of the audience at each show and in each town. A "straw house" in which all the seats are sold out, brings joy throughout the circus community.

While larger circuses start the season with an almost complete schedule of sites and performance dates, mud shows do not have a long range date book. They distribute route sheets month by month, so most of the personnel are not sure where they will be past the current State.[13] Smaller circuses travel every day or every other day. Larger circuses can stay from five to fifteen days in a single venue.

Some of this demanding pace is peculiar to circuses in the United States. People who come from other countries for the higher

---

13   A survey of part of one season in an East Coast circus demonstrates the span of movement. March was spent in Florida, Georgia, and North Carolina on 24 sites. April meant 27 sites in North Carolina and Virginia, May, 30 sites in Virginia, Maryland, Delaware, Pennsylvania, and West Virginia, with one dark day of no shows on Mother's Day. June through October followed the pattern of about 28 sites per month and covered Ohio, Massachusetts, Vermont, New Hampshire, Maine, and Connecticut before reversing the tour from North to South. The number of shows on this tour was forty per month. In a comparable time period one of Ringling's units covered only thirty-two sites not the approximately one hundred ninety-two visited by the smaller circus.

salaries paid here, find the schedule particularly difficult. In some South American countries, a circus can stay in one town for a month or more. There is more of a chance to get to know some of the local people, to discover the facilities available in the area, and to accomplish the mundane tasks of everyday life. One young woman said, "We travel so much. We travel more than we are in the shows. Three days on the road and four days in town. New Jersey today, Texas next. The only problem here in America is we travel so much. In Mexico and Europe, you stay one month or more in a town. You can get your own church, get to know people. We didn't know it was so tough here. The difference is the money. They pay better here."[14]

Performers who have come from European circuses tell of a similar, more relaxed rhythm of life. Speaking at a Circus and Traveling Show Ministry Conference, Aurelia Nock recalled her childhood with her grandmother Canastrelli's circus. They would summer in Naples and winter in Sicily. Their major travel concern was to get back by September, since they had to travel across the sea by ferry with the horses and supplies.[15]

But business demands affect the tenor of life in a circus in the United States. Large circuses may be unionized and the stresses of maintaining the payroll, equipment, and travel expenses of a large corporate endeavor can make performers feel that the front office is sacrificing the quality of the show and the quality of life of the performers for the sake of the bottom line.[16] Small circuses can also be viewed as harsh on their employees because the low net income keeps salaries down and work loads up. Those overseeing the circus have their own difficulties. A retired manager discussed the stress involved, "It was not like being a performer or a worker.... You had to be on duty twenty-four hours."

---

14   On mud circuses in the United States a worker might be getting $150 a week plus gas and meals. There are no health or other benefits on these smaller shows. The Big Apple and Ringling Circuses are ones who pay larger salaries but they are by no means high wages. Union workers in these shows do get benefits and some vacation time during the season.
15   Aurelia Nock joined the Ringling Circus in 1954 from Italy along with her family, The Canastrelli Troupe. She married Eugene Nock from Switzerland and they raised four boys, who are all in the circus business.
16   Performers are contracted for the run of a show, one or two years maximum. Those in other types of work in the circus may not need to renew their contracts each year if they are part of a collective bargaining union. Union representatives renegotiate their members' contracts collectively for longer periods of time. In addition to having some workers with union salaries and benefits, large circuses use ticketing services which, while more efficient, also add to the ticket price.

Even within the larger entertainment world of the United States, circus schedules are considered grueling. One outside video company employee on loan to one of the bigger circuses made some comparisons with other performance groups with whom he has traveled. "On a normal (non-circus) tour, there's about three to five shows a week. A five-show week would be very busy for normal entertainment, normal Rock tours. Here we do between nine and thirteen." The family ethos of the circus, however, is experienced as a counter-balance to the spirit-sapping work schedule. This same respondent has found at least one other person who shares his faith and with whom he can occasionally discuss the Scripture. He found this a new experience compared to other work assignments. As he explained, "In this entertainment business you are almost looked down on for being spiritual. It is like, 'How can you believe in God.'"

However the physical challenges are significant. With the schedule of circuses in the US, even fitting in necessary household maintenance becomes an extreme challenge. One has little time to seek out a Laundromat, find a way to get to and from the facility, and just do one's wash. Shopping, finding medical care and other necessities can be emotionally and physically taxing. Some have mentioned the strain all of this places on being spiritually aware. One man told me, "It is a merry-go-round that doesn't stop and you have to run, run, run and jump on to it. And it's just relentless. You don't get time to breathe and absorb and smell the flowers and all the stuff that you need for balance in your life."

If a circus has a train, it is often parked far from town. Then the circus does provide a midnight shuttle run to an all night supermarket about once a week for those who do not have transportation. But for those in other companies, it can be hard to get the simple things like soap and tissues. Those without their own vehicles depend on others to take them to find a place to wash their clothes, to see the local sights on occasion, to visit an available doctor, or to go anywhere else off the lot.

Dark days, days with no shows and no travel, are few and far between. This type of demanding schedule leads to a great deal of stress, especially as the season progresses and circus folk become more physically worn from the intense work and travel schedule.

Circus Life

Yet, many circus people live an evident spiritual life while enduring a highly pressured schedule of movement and performance in tight living quarters. Circus life is remarkably structured in its frequent movement, heavy performance schedule, and restricted living space. 1/3 of those who participated in my study mentioned the busy schedule, amount of work, and travel schedule as significant factors of circus life which make it harder to live a spiritual life. Others said these very factors impel one to have a spiritual base. A thirty-two year old woman explained, "there is so much going on that you have to have a foundation to keep yourself sane. ...Even if I can't get on my knees, I constantly say "Thank you." I am grateful for this opportunity. I am trying to do the best I can with what I have."

People who live and work in the circus choose a migratory existence. In community with others they travel from place to place to bring their performance to others along the road. It is a life considered far from ordinary and yet it is followed by people whose spiritual desires resonate with many who do not share their lifestyle.

While smaller circuses can consist of thirty to fifty workers, larger shows can have more than 300 people on the payroll. Within this range, there are two main divisions of circuses: mud circuses and indoor circuses. Mud circuses perform under tents erected outdoors. Once made of canvas but now more frequently constructed of vinyl, the tents are set up on dirt or asphalt lots. The term mud circus comes from the frequent wet conditions in which they set up as they move either every day or every other day in a new town. A bad lot can make everyone's tasks more difficult.

Indoor circuses use small or large arenas. They customize their rigging to establish performance rings within those structures for a week or more at a time.[17]

Whether moving every day or every week, the cycle of circus life is very similar, i.e., move, load in (set up), perform, load out (take down), and move again. This continues for a full season of

---

17   Some of the bigger circuses, including Ringling Brothers, Big Apple, and Cirque du Soleil, are particularly well known because they rent arenas in large cities where the venues can hold large numbers of people at every performance. Cirque du Soleil also has some almost permanent shows which remain in one location and do not travel for years at a time. Because it often does not follow the migrant model, Cirque du Soleil is not referenced in most of the material included here.

nine and a half to eleven months a year. It can be an exhausting schedule. In one of their first letters after joining the circus, Sisters Dorothy and Bernard wrote, "The best cure for insomnia is working on the circus."[18] After months of this hard work there is the much anticipated move to Winter Quarters. It is the end of the circuit and by then everyone is bone tired.

Indoor circuses have a break from performance for about one month at the end of the year, during which time they are normally preparing for and practicing a new show. One performer described his family's activities in-between seasons, "It is practicing, getting equipment together, getting ready for the next time we go out."

Because there is no salary for performers during this time and money can run out quickly, some artists who have their own acts hire agents to book them for shows in between circus seasons. Others may pick up limited engagement performance opportunities on their own, or do some alternative work. Victoria Rossi remembers winter dates filled in with Shrine circus dates and benefit performances in heated buildings, whose concrete floors were more dangerous for her family's various acts.[19] In her memoir, acclaimed horseback rider Dorothy Herbert speaks of teaching others to ride during the break time.[20]

Mundane concerns that cannot be tended to during the rest of the year are also managed during winter quarters. These include doctors' appointments which are almost impossible to schedule while on the road.

Mud shows have a longer break because outdoor lots are not suitable for use as early in the year. When they return to Winter Quarters they do not close shop immediately because time is needed to dry out the tent and clean-up for about five days before having a party to celebrate a completed season. Their break is closer to ten weeks or a little more. However, it is worth mentioning that circus folks are not paid during their time in between shows.

---

18   Sr. Dorothy Fabritze, *MSC Circus Journal*, (April 12, 2000).
19   Victoria Rossi. *Spangles, Elephants, Violets and Me: The Circus Inside Out*, (New York: iUniverse, 2007) 20.
20   Dorothy Herbert. *Dorothy Herbert: A Memoir – Riding Sensation of the Age, A Memoir*. (Televast, Fl: Dale A. Riker, 2005).

Once the show gets on the road, a day off is a rare experience. In fact one man described days with only one show as "a little vacation." For weekly indoor shows this means travel on Monday,[21] load in on Tuesday, rehearsal and warm up stretches early Wednesday,[22] and then a show on Wednesday night, two on Thursday, two on Friday, and two or three on both Saturday and Sunday. After that it is time for load out on Sunday night.

On mud circuses, the schedule is tighter: Load in on Monday morning, rehearse and stretch, two performances, load out and move Monday night, load in on Tuesday, rehearse and stretch, two performances, load out and move Tuesday night, etc. or Load in Monday, two performances, stay overnight, two performances on Tuesday, then load out and move Tuesday night. In either type of circus, there is a tremendous organizational effort needed to make a success of all the setting up, breaking down, and completing the jump to the next location.

Then, after driving all night, it is not uncommon to be without running water and electricity, which means, for example, no shower, until sometime the next day or later when the utilities are hooked up.

Some travel in the morning instead of night but the routine is the same, seven days a week, forty-two to forty-eight weeks a year. The only day off is a dark day, meaning a day when they were not able to secure a performance space. This may be a physical relief but it means that the circus owner will have a harder time meeting payroll and those on the circus may have to wait another week until they can get paid.

Here is one male roustabout's account of a typical day: "Up at 5:30 a.m., coffee, hit the road following the arrows to the next town. 8:30-9:00 began helping drive stakes (using a mechanical stake driver) 10:30 stretch out the canvas and tie it off to the stakes. Then 20 minutes break for breakfast...When the boss whistled we started to pop up the tent - push the poles into place. As soon as the seat wagons were pulled in – unfolded them, finishing about 12:30,

---

21 For short jumps one man said, "If you are in early, you can do the town on Monday."
22 Even though the same show is repeated day after day, roughly 400 shows a year in large circuses, a rehearsal is needed at each new venue. The dimensions of the arena determine the shape and size of the performance rings, entrance opening and positions, etc. Unfamiliarity with the location of an entry space into the ring has caused occasionally serious falls.

lunch, shower and nap. 4:30 show time, different jobs, concessions, front door, and Midway hustler. 10 p.m. tear down the tent, usually done by 12:00."

On a bigger circus, many jobs are more defined but no less packed with activity.[23] A boss clown said, "My days are full and busy. I'm in charge of fifteen clowns, nine dogs and myself - Daily chores, PR events, performance, production meetings, travel and exercise." Publicizing the circus is something which includes more than printed advertisements. Once on location, there are visits planned to radio and television stations to promote the show. There are interviews scheduled with newspaper journalists and other media reporters. In some cases someone may also drive a circus truck around town playing circus music on a calliope or over amplified speakers to announce the show location and times.

Those not directly involved with the show may have a less demanding schedule. A nineteen year old who works in the nursery at one circus has the morning off.[24] She does housework, prepares meals for later, and goes to the bank and stores before she begins her workday. However, her regimen is not the norm. A former Controller for one of the Ringling units[25] mentioned that he had, "Office work seven days a week for about sixty-five hours per week."[26] A woman who prepares meals for the show folks says she spends, "twelve to fourteen hours a day in the cookhouse."

---

23   Gender differences in employment do not appear to be significant in many areas of circus life. Both men and women performers generally have strong bodies whose well defined muscles have been honed in the development of their athletic skills. All are costumed in ways meant to display their graceful forms and dazzle the eye of the beholder. Men and women handle animals. Ringmasters and clowns are disproportionately but not exclusively male. Male clowns sometimes impersonate female characters. Concessions are sold by women and men alike but other backstage jobs are weighted more toward one gender than another. The majority of stagehands are male. The majority of those caring for costumes are female. There are male and female counterparts in many management positions but the balance leans more to the male side.
24   Ringling Brothers Circus provides a nursery for its employees. It accommodates the many families who need supervision of their little ones during work hours.
25   As of this writing the veteran Ringling Brothers Circus, in its 140th season in 2010, has three separate units. Two troupes, the Red and the Blue units, alternate every other year in the same large city arenas. The Gold unit is scheduled for smaller venues and does some work in countries outside the United States as well.
26   A current office manager outlines some of his duties, "I settle with sponsors, pay bills, stuff pay envelopes, count money, work on computers, sometimes sell tickets, and perform other office chores. I drive my rig from town to town. Off hours are for laundry, buying groceries, going to the bank or post office, etc. Other office work might include collecting the log books from the show's commercial drivers or keeping records of how long animals travel on the train, to insure adequate rest stops.

A forty-five year old who does electrical work and takes care of props says his routine on non-travel days, "starts at 6:00 a.m. and ends at 1:00 a.m. the next day, with intervals of rest of about five hours a day."[27]

A seventh-generation thirty-one year old female described her day, with performances at 4:00 pm and 7:00 pm: "Well, I woke up about 5:30 a.m., loaded the elephants up, traveled, got to the lot, unloaded around 9:00 a.m., set up the elephants' pen, started cooking in the cookhouse, set up the tent while everyone ate, washed the animals, took a shower, got ready for the show, make-up, wig, got tickets to sell at the door, did rides, then cooked for dinner, did the show and after the show, took the tent down, relaxed with friends and went to bed."[28]

Another circus person takes it all in stride, however, and said that his life is, "normal, like any other common and ordinary person. I work, exercise, have fun, with the exception that I travel a lot."

This is a true migrant life where one lives on the road, either in a house trailer, a train, or in a truck. When the circus stakes are pulled up, so is your home, and it is moved to the next parking lot or train yard.

There are approximately four thousand people living and working in circuses in the United States. Some people in the circus are seekers of a general sort who do not have a defined relationship to God. One man said he does not specifically think about God but, he said, "I think of the history of God. I think of man's interpretation of God."

There are also some people who choose not to follow a spiritual path in the circus. Although the lifestyle seems to shape the response to God and sacred realities among believers and seekers, it is not the cause of spirituality. People of various faiths and people of no faith live and work together in ways similar to that in most other circumstances in pluralistic societies.

---

27 This native Spanish speaker uses his free time to teach Math and English to children and adult artists on the show.
28 A former business manager told me that what you want in an elephant trainer is someone who wants to be there for the elephants, who will come to them whether they are paid or not. Whether you shush them out or not they keep coming back, they want to be with the elephants.

And despite the many positive communal elements of life in the circus, it is not without its negative elements as well. Some young women complain of inappropriate sexual advances by some of the men on the circus. This is a problem for these women as women. It also has additional religious dimensions for some of the women.

The circus is a community which includes members of diverse faith traditions: Christians, Jews, Muslims, and Buddhists all coexist and seek ways to live out their religious commitments in the circus world. When being encouraged to become intimate with one of the other workers, one 28-year old said, "I tell them no because I am a Muslim and I don't do that." From that same religious perspective there are other aspects of the life that some Muslims find difficult. For example, having men regularly being in the presence of women wearing the sometimes scanty costumes used by performers can be experienced as a threat to religious fidelity.

Following religious prescriptions are also difficult but staying faithful is still possible. One 29-year old man described the importance of going to the Mosque, praying at set times, and reading the Qur'an, all of which are often not possible. He concluded, however, by saying, "Practicing it is difficult here. Living it is not. It's always there."

So, even with so many challenging circumstances, most circus people find a way to stay close to God. 95% of those who responded to the survey reported that they pray and a striking 90% followed up that statement by saying that they pray frequently or all the time. A thirty-nine year old woman who said that she thinks of God "all the time," added, "before work, after work. My husband and I pray before the show to protect everybody. I feel as though we have a good connection."

A fifty-year old man shared, "I pray formally in the morning and at night and I talk with my Heavenly father constantly during the day." Another said, "I think of the Lord when I wake in the morning and am on my knees. I am in prayer all day long and before I retire for the night, again on my knees in prayer."

Quite a few people talked about their prayer as a conversation in which they talk to God whom they experience as being present with them. A fifty-one year old woman wrote, "God is my heavenly Father and Jesus is my best friend and I seek the guidance of the Holy Spirit in ALL THINGS!" A thirty-nine year old woman said, "I talk to God like he's standing right there, my best friend in the whole world....I just know that he's there."[29] A sixty-two year old woman noted, "I just talk. I thank God for the good and grumble about the bad."

Others also mention praying at a minimum in the morning and night, "for every performance and for traveling to the next town." Some use devotionals on a regular basis, and things that happen throughout the day prompt them, in one thirty-eight year old man's words "to think and give praise." Though only 26.9% of them are able to join in community worship frequently or regularly on the road, 88% said that there are things about the circus that help them stay close to God. Remaining sensitive to the holy and being spiritually alert, requires commitment and creativity.

Circus people adapt their spiritual practices to fit the migrant nature of their life. There are many relationships between their physical and spiritual experiences. For example, no access to a sacred building leads to the creation of sacred space wherever they agree to focus on God, frequent movement from place to place is coupled with an unmovable rootedness in God's presence, repetition of a highly structured performance depends on flexibility of roles among those who present the show, and isolation from the broader society is counterbalanced by the essential interdependence within the circus community.

---

29   A number of respondents referred to God as a friend or their best friend. Many also expressed equal comfort in praying with gratitude, requests for assistance, or expressions of complaint.

CHAPTER 2

Where the Community Gathers is Sacred Space

> *"The Lord appeared to Abraham near the great trees of Mamre while he was sitting at the entrance to his tent in the heat of the day. Abraham looked up and saw three men standing nearby. When he saw them, he hurried from the entrance of his tent and bowed low to the ground." (Genesis 18:1-2)*

Performers mill around in the empty arena before the doors are opened to the ticket holders. Lithe dancers limber up with improbable stretches or stand around chatting in their fantastic costumes. As show time approaches, one young woman at the edge of the ring lifts her head a bit. This silent signal has a magnetic effect as, in ones and twos, others drift toward her and a small circle forms. The dancers begin to pray. They praise God for God's greatness and love. They ask God to protect the performers and to bless those in the audience. Then, as they conclude, the doors open and the show begins.

Backstage, an athletic horseback rider stands in the stall before his saddled stallion. Straight and focused, he holds his hands together, waist high, palms upward and prays the 4 o'clock prayer of faithful Muslims. Then he swings up onto his horse and joins his troupe speeding toward the curtain and into the arena.

At the same time not ten feet away divided only by a glass door five young children glue together a foam representation of the Last Supper as part of their preparation sessions for First Eucharist.

A half hour later, that same room has been rearranged to accommodate performers in their changing robes, stage crew workers, and other circus folks who gather in the 35 minutes between shows for a rare opportunity to celebrate Eucharist. A local parish priest smiles and images Jesus, who draws all things to himself, drawing all of the circus people to himself at this very moment. He suggests that God may well be using the gifts of each person present to heal those with sad spirits who are among those who come to each performance. The eyes of those assembled for Eucharist light up. The visitor has recognized and affirmed their share in Christ's mission to bring God's love to the world.

In the circus, sacred space is created where the community gathers. It is created by the faith of the believers, who identify the divine in their midst. Sacred space is not limited to a physical area or a building set aside for the community to gather. It is wherever the all-embracing divine life is encountered. It is the place where one stops in the middle of the workday to listen to God. It is the ordinary transformed. It is the experience of Moses, who, while leading his father-in-law's flocks "to the far side of the wilderness," came upon a blazing bush. There he responded to the divine call to take off his shoes "for the place on which you stand is holy ground." (Exodus 3:1-5) The physical dimensions did not make the location sacred space; it was the encounter with the ever-present divine in that common place which made it holy ground.

Circus space, while also limited in area, can readily become a sacred space. Traveling with one's home means that one's household must be relatively compact. The inevitable limitations of a moveable living area can engender a unique appreciation of and reverence for that space as holy ground, especially when physical structures designated as places of prayer and community worship are unavailable on a regular basis.

Formal religious communities are rare in the circus world. Individuals often are officially members of a specific religion, e.g.,

Catholic, Lutheran, Evangelical, Muslim, or Jewish.[30] However, many have little connection with an individual congregation while they are on the road. Spiritual formation sessions and religious services are not available in most circus settings. 45% of the survey respondents have either never attended any talk, class, or faith-sharing session or have not done so since their youth. 20% do so when they are off the road or when the sisters offer a learning/sharing opportunity.

Some have put such concerns out of their minds since they have no way to change the situation. Others have faded away from religious practice. Many, however, remain consciously hungry for religious connections of some form or another. They are a migrant people, on the move, with no traveling parish, synagogue, congregation, or mosque.

One thirty-seven year old woman who was interviewed said, "God is not only in church. There is often no church around the building. Sometimes I hear church bells and pray or I go in to visit."

Another woman close in age lamented, "Sadly we cannot go to Mass often. God is with you as long as you can pray. You can pray when you are in the building or on the train. On vacations, when we can, we go to church, sometimes just to show our daughters the inside of the church if there is no service at that time."

For most involved in this study, spiritual hunger is evident. They pray individually, express a desire for spiritual growth and deeper knowledge of God, make the time for faith sharing and religious formation when they can find like-minded companions or spiritual guides, and, take advantage of worship opportunities when they are made available. Whether an official religious minister is present in a circus or not, circus folk's spiritual life finds some expression. One flamboyant headlining acrobat always makes the sign of the cross before beginning his daring act. When a particular performance was sold out to a group who did not want to see any religious gestures, the star refused to perform. His spiritually symbolic action was too significant for him to give up for even one show.

---

30 An estimated 40% of the combined circus and carnival population are Catholics according to the National Conference of Catholic Bishops. In my survey 14% of the respondents did not indicate their religion, 63.5% identified themselves as Catholic, 1.6% as Orthodox, and 17.5% as Christians of other denominations. 3.2% said they were Muslim.

In quieter sections of the arena, Muslim workers regularly stop throughout the day to turn their thoughts to God, though their desire to kneel for these prayers is rarely possible.

Physical devotional objects experienced as indicators of a connection to the sacred were mentioned a number of times in survey responses. In some cases, there are indications that the use of these sensible objects was a stepping stone to a more transcendent awareness of the divine. This is one kind of transformational result of using the spiritual symbols. Another effect is that their presence is a type of incarnational experience of the mystery of God. Physical reminders provide an opportunity to connect with the eternal underpinnings of otherwise mundane realities. There did not seem to be a sense of dependency on these physical representations. People did not appear to turn to them as if the devotional objects themselves held the spiritual reality to which they are meant to point. Rather those talking about crosses, rosaries, and icons gave the impression that these concrete symbols were aids to spiritual awareness.

One performer spoke of a reminder of God she takes with her into the center ring, "I have a small medal for prayer inside my costume." This phrasing is significant in the sense that she spoke of the medal as being a means to move her toward prayer, not as though it were for protection, as though it were a charm or superstition of some sort.

Although some circus members agree with the man who said, "I don't need any item that reminds me of God. It's simply my faith that makes me believe in Him," and the young woman who considered, "I don't need anything to remind me. I used to. Now everything reminds me of God." Other circus folks have physical reminders of God's presence in their living quarters and/or in their vehicles.

A fifty-three year old woman said, "I always pray. I have a little scapular[31] by my pillow. I kiss it when I get up in the morning.... The fact that we move so much on highways often gives you closeness

---

31 A scapular is a devotional object worn by some Catholics. Derived from a full-length part of the attire worn by members of monastic communities, it is a rectangular, double-sided cloth reminder of a pledge to live a certain spiritual way of life.

to Him...We travel so much, I always pray before we go anywhere in the car. I have a rosary hanging from the mirror to remind me to pray." Several other women and men mentioned having a rosary to help remind them of God, including a fifteen decade rosary that one young woman's dad gave her when she returned to the circus for a second year and a rosary that one young woman puts "on the car mirror of the person whose car we use."

Quite a few circus folks mentioned having a cross in their homes or on their persons. One woman said, "I keep a cross to bless our home. We pray before meals. We are grateful. I make the Sign of the Cross when leaving the house, to ask God's blessing." A forty-five year old crew member and both a thirty-one year old and nineteen-year old woman each mentioned having a cross which they take everywhere. A sixty five year old man said he and his wife "keep palms that have been blessed on Palm Sunday and a blessed crucifix on the wall of our travel trailer." Others mentioned having images of the Holy Trinity, Jesus, Mary, Nativity scenes, angels, and certain saints. One mother had given her son a bracelet that he wears all the time. "It is a circle of pictures of saints and Jesus on wood." Although many of those surveyed do not have any particular religious materials and do not feel a need for any, others use sensible objects to remind them of God's presence. One young woman said, "Sometimes we need something to touch. To hold onto."

Speaking of popular spiritual traditions which are part of the Mexican heritage, Virgilio Elizondo, gives a positive interpretation of many religious expressions. "For us, these experiences are simply *nuestra vida de fe!* They are our own sacramental life which has arisen out of the common priesthood of the people acting in the power of the Spirit."[32]

In their nomadic life style, circus people have developed a sense of the sacredness of space. Dislocated from a stable faith community, some do, however, seek out formal sacred spaces on their route. A sampling of the circus people's own reflections on sacred space illustrates their experiences.

---

32   Virgilio Elizondo. "Popular Religion as the Core of Cultural Identity Based on the Mexican American Experience in the United States," in *American Spiritualities: A Reader*, edited by Catherine L. Albanese, (Bloomington, Indiana: Indiana University Press, 2001) 95-111.)

"I try to visit local churches of my denomination (Episcopal) when possible."

"If I have a friend who has a car and knows where a Mosque is, I might go, if there is time. When we are in places for a month of shows, Chicago, New York, Florida, I take a bus or car with friends and pray at a Mosque."

One infrequent church goer reported, "I know different families that were on this show, you know you get in at two in the morning and they are up at six o'clock to go to church, in a town where they have no idea where they are going."

"As soon as we go to a city, we go to Church before we start working."

"I try to find time but it is hard. Sometimes we go to a Russian Church when we are in big cities, about four times a year and we light candles. There is a big Russian Church in Baltimore that we can go to on Monday or Tuesday. We can understand the Russian priest."

One exception to the rule was a traveling group called The Circus Kingdom which traveled for twelve years doing two sixteen-week seasonal tours in summer and Christmastime. Formed by a minister and his wife, the ecumenical troupe was fashioned as a type of "faith sharing group" which sought to spread the Gospel message through circus performance. The young people, usually about twenty-five college students on vacation, who signed on to be part of the tour could count on regular prayer opportunities. Now retired, the woman, a nurse who ran the circus with her husband, talked about their practice of "circling up" before the first show of each day. "One performer would volunteer to say a prayer. Most of the time I found these prayers very meaningful and thoughtful.... Every Sunday we had a church service. If the sponsor was a church, then we went to that church or, if we were not sponsored by a church, then we designed and had our own church service....At one of our Circus Kingdom reunions we worshipped in a synagogue....We spent a week with Hoxie Brothers Circus when they were performing in the Bahamas. There my husband held a church service in the tent for the performers and employees."[33] However, even this devoted believer gained a new insight to prayer during her travels: "Throughout my tours with the Circus Kingdom, I learned that you weren't just limited to special prayers in church, but God was available all the time, anywhere…always listening."

For the majority of people finding a house of worship is not the norm. The work load and tight schedule are most frequently given as the reasons why people do not attend local religious services on the road. A twenty-nine year old Muslim man who cares for some of the animals regretted, "I can't do the special five times a day prayer. I have no time. My father takes a day off to pray with others in a mosque on holidays but I can't because of my job." A twenty-year old Catholic woman said, "In the circus, one doesn't have time to go to Mass."

A forty-four year old man said that he does not join in the services even when they are offered on site. "I pray every day…I don't go to services….Busy as we are, and we get forty-five minutes between shows and the service is between shows and it's about forty minutes long, and there's no time to eat or anything else, and I probably should go."

Even a priest who worked in the circus for awhile said, "…the heavy work schedule and no free time makes formal prayer difficult. Also, it is a real chore to find the church in a strange town." But this does not mean they become disconnected from the divine presence. An eighteen-year old woman said, "I can't go to church on Sundays and I can't participate in Mass, so I have to do more thinking about God." About going to services, a thirty-seven year old said, "Sometimes I don't have time but I have time with Papa God every night."

A twenty-seven year old woman from Mexico regretted that the circus schedule in the United States requires work or travel everyday which makes it almost impossible to get to church. However, she added, "It doesn't matter if there is one or two or three persons, that's the church. My boyfriend believes in God, every night he prays…so we get together and do that together." More than one person asserted that nothing prevents them from being close to God or continuing in their faith.

---

33 A former worker in the Circus Kingdom reminisced, "It was all about getting close to God and sharing Him with others. The circus brought me to where I am today."

Some young people mentioned that being away from their families for the first time has created new challenges. One South American woman explained, "We are alone, away from country, religious family where church was close and it was all easy. You always had someone to show you which way to go. Now you have to know which is right and wrong." Being on their own has made them realize that a decision to continue their faith is completely up to them. It is between them and God. Given those circumstances, one said, "You really have to decide, I will follow God with all my heart." Another added, "I know I'll come out with a much stronger relationship with God."

Spiritual seekers in the circus are often willing to go to great lengths to strengthen their relationship with God. Thirty-nine percent of the people in my survey indicated that they do attend religious services when the Sisters on their circus arrange for a priest to say Mass or when there is a priest working on the circus.[34] One woman who tries to go to parish liturgies on the road when she can says, "Of course we usually feel like 'strangers' at a local parish, and we are and are very appreciative when we can celebrate in our circus family."

Not all of those who attend the circus Masses are Catholic but they come to share in a common public worship experience. One fifty-three year old woman said, "It is a fantastic opportunity when a service is held here at the circus. Most people don't go to things but they will go to a barbeque and they will always go if there is Mass here." One young Protestant woman said, "I am not Catholic but I tend to go to Mass. There is very good stuff there. It is all that is offered to me so I take advantage of it."

A forty-seven year old woman told of a recent Mass held in the circus cook house. For her, "It was a joy."

Not everyone is equally committed to the process, however. One thirty-seven year old woman said, "When there is Mass here, I go sometimes. Sometimes instead I am thinking about going to the Pie Cart to get something to eat."[35] During a Spring interview, a

---

34 A priest who spent some time in the circus remarked, "People were always eager for Mass when I was with the show. "Missa, padre?" I was overwhelmed by the people that would gather, ecumenical."
35 The Pie Cart is the on-site food vending stand for circus workers to buy their meals, if they wish.

thirty-one year old woman told me how difficult it is to go to Mass on the road. She continued, "So the last time I went to Mass was Christmas....Sister Dorothy and Sister Bernard arrange for a priest to come, I think it works out to be once a month or sometimes more. When they arrange to have Mass here, I certainly try. I haven't gotten to every single one of them but I try to make an effort to come to those."

In order to celebrate Eucharist, those attending take the only half hour they have in-between shows to come together for Mass. When that is possible and before it can begin, a priest has to be located who is willing and able to come at the available time slot, an unused room has to be found for the liturgy, and those who might be interested have to be informed. Lacking an established sacred building they consecrate a temporary space, blessing it by their desire for union with God in that place.

I have attended a number of these services which take place in a room borrowed for the brief gathering or at an entryway with participants sitting on the stairs in their costumes and work clothes and the presider facing them at the bottom of the steps. Young people take out the Mass supply box and cover whatever table can be found with an altar cloth, and set out bread and wine. Some members read from the Scriptures in either Spanish or English and occasionally someone will sing a spontaneous hymn after Communion. Then it is back off to work or to have a quick bite to eat before the next performance. The priest is asked to linger a few moments for those who would like to talk to him, ask for special prayers, or celebrate Reconciliation. They lean together on the hallway wall a few paces away from the hustling workers bringing the props in for the next opening act.[36]

Good Friday is usually a busy performance day and when folks are looking for a chance to reflect on that solemn day, the Sisters have been known to set up a circle of folding chairs and set out copies of the Good Friday readings and prayers. In between their performances and other responsibilities, those who choose to sit in for as long as they can in the small group's remembrance

---

36 One generous Portuguese priest in Newark, New Jersey gave his address to some Brazilian performers. Five or six of them got together when they had a few hours and went to his parish for Reconciliation and Mass. Afterwards he invited them home for a meal with Brazilian food. With obvious delight, they told me, "He spoke our language."

of the Passion of Christ. Those who join the sacred circle are able to take turns reading aloud. A single continuous prayer service is sustained by a fluctuating band of believers.

Adaptations are often necessary. Many circus people are part of families whose children are with them on the road. As in all families, this means that, at least on occasion, the youngsters find creative solutions to unexpected challenges. In one sacramental celebration, in a borrowed and barren box of a room, it was a child who transformed the setting. He had just completed his First Reconciliation and returned to the group of youngsters and their families who had gathered for the celebration. Remembering that he should spend some private time in prayer talking to Jesus after the encounter, he glanced around the room and silently walked to a corner where he promptly knelt down facing the walls for his private words of thanks to Jesus. One by one the children followed his example by spending quiet time kneeling in a corner for prayer before returning to their companions. Then the adults present were welcomed to celebrate Reconciliation as well. When the child's father, a headlining acrobat known for his swagger and dramatic feats of daring, had completed his own confession, he, too, followed his son's example and took a turn kneeling in the corner so recently established as a place of prayer. That space retained its sacred status throughout the celebration as one after the other of the adults knelt on the floor's bare surface and then returned to the folding chairs where the community was gathered.

Sometimes people celebrating sacraments will wear the special clothing that is often associated with those events. They will often find a way to get a white suit or white dress for their youngster who is receiving Jesus in the Eucharist for the first time. With no external obligation to wear certain clothes, they take the initiative to help create a spiritual atmosphere for the sacred celebration which is taking place in an otherwise plain setting.

Father Dick Notter, who visits various circuses throughout the year to offer spiritual ministry recalls an invitation he received to celebrate five baptisms at the same time. It was to take place in a home during the winter break and Father Notter arranged to do a baptismal catechesis for the parents the day before the sacrament. He was quite surprised that over forty people arrived for the instruction, all eager to hear what he had to say. Arriving the next day for the celebration, he was again overwhelmed. The people had emptied the small house of all its furniture in order to decorate it as a chapel for the event. They created the sacred space that fit their understanding of the sacred ritual they were to celebrate.

One interesting phenomenon among those who are on the road most of the year is that many remain deeply connected to their home congregation located in their winter quarters, which for many circus folks is Sarasota Florida.[37]

St. Martha's Catholic Church, a large parish with five daily Masses, weekly Masses in Vietnamese, Spanish, Latin, and English, is served by seven resident priests. This Sarasota, Florida parish has remained the spiritual home for many contemporary circus families whose grandparents helped raise the funds to build the present church.[38] Early in its history, the parish's pastor, Father Elslander reached out to the circus community. During the same year that the parish was officially established, John Ringling moved his circus's winter quarters from Connecticut to Florida. The new pastor of recently created St. Martha's embraced the Church's new neighbors, the Ringling Brothers and Barnum and Bailey Circus.[39] Sarasota's population swelled between seasons with circus performers and roustabouts. For their part, over many years, circus folks organized an annual performance on the Church's grounds as a fund raiser for the parish.

This religious community remains the hub of life for many retired circus folks as well as the spiritual home base for others between touring seasons.[40] Some participants mentioned being

---

37 Although some circus workers continue to live in their travel trailers or RV's, others rent apartments nearby, and many over time have purchased homes to use as their Winter Quarters. When this trend began, Sarasota enacted rules insuring that tract sizes were large enough to park trailers and to tend animals with sufficient space. Although Ringling Brothers has its winter quarters in Florida, other circuses choose different areas of the country to spend their time in-between seasons. Some who are from outside the United States return to their home country for at least some of the time between tours.
38 St. Martha's Church décor reflects its close ties to the circus community. Antique circus wagon wheels adorn the sanctuary and the organ.
39 Early in its history, John Ringling North of Ringling Brothers and Barnum and Bailey Circus joined with Father Elslander, the pastor of St. Martha's, to have the priest bless the circus trains as they started out on the road each season. That tradition continues to this day.
40 One retired circus performer who is among the 7th generation of her family to work in circus, continues her involvement by making vestments and liturgical items for the circus ministry. She said, "I pray with every stitch."

married at St. Martha's. Others referred to having their children baptized there. One retired circus matriarch has four children. The family celebrated three of the Christenings at St. Martha's. Travel schedules, however, meant that the fourth child was baptized during the World Fair in Flushing, New York.[41]

The current pastor of St. Martha's, Father Fausto Stampiglia, SAC, debated as a young person whether he should become a priest or a circus clown. He chose to become a priest who ministers to and with circus folks.

One non-denominational Evangelical circus person told me "There is a big church in Sarasota. It is the Mother Church, Iglesias de los Hermanos. I go there once in a while with my brother and sister. Usually I go to the small one near my home."

Another woman goes so far as to continue to have ten percent of her salary taken out and sent to a savings account so that she will be able to give her tithe when she returns home. She believes it is her responsibility to support the spread of the Word. She added, "Jesus is the biggest part of my life. He keeps me going."

Several respondents said, "When I am home during the winter, I attend church regularly." And one forty-four year old man added, "There's been plenty of times I have returned home on a Sunday morning at seven am and then been sitting at Mass at eleven am."

Another man said, "It is part of our practice as a family to be part of a church....It's very important to belong someplace and we are not free agents. It makes us answerable to each other"

Only twenty percent of the survey participants indicated that they never, rarely, or only sometimes take part in community worship experiences.

But there are many other sources of spiritual awareness to supplement the less than regular opportunities for shared worship. One nineteen-year old finds God's presence in her work in the nursery. "I take care of children. That's a reminder that there's somebody there helping me and He needs my help."

---

[41] Victoria Cristiani Rossi was baptized by Monsignor Elslander, the first pastor of St. Martha's in 1940 just before the circus train left for the opening of a new season.

Traveling also provides an opportunity to experience one's surroundings as sacred space. There is a great expanse which encompasses those on the road. The trailers and trucks wend their way across the lonely desert of Arizona, through the winding mountain roads of Colorado, and along the busy highways of California and New Jersey. And on those journeys they are exposed to the grandeur and diversity of the country's landscape. It is easy to understand that another sacred space for many on the circus is the one shared with all those who respond to the wonders of creation. It is in nature itself. Whether in those terrains through which the caravan passes or in those where the travelers set up their tent, the created world often provides a space to reflect and pray.

A fifty-five-year old man said, "I think about God continually in the daily tasks of work....Then in the sights along the way that we have the opportunity to observe and at night when I look at the stars and whenever I think of my family."

Another man, age fifty-eight described experiences which initiate thought of God, "Animals, nature is a Big One, lakes, forests, ocean, the country, the earth in general."

The power of nature keeps one sixty-three year old woman close to God. She couldn't fully complete her description, "The severity of the weather makes you realize what a small part you are....When you are under a tornado watch and the clouds are boiling over you over there and you are sitting in a ditch over here, it, you know."

A man of forty four when asked if he ever thinks of God reflected, "Especially when we are traveling, you sit there and just look at how big everything is and how beautiful everything is. And it's like, this did not just happen."

A thirty-nine-year old woman when asked if and when she thinks of God said, "I find something everyday. I see God's presence in the beautiful trees; I see God's presence everywhere."

Others spoke of "beautiful vistas," "lovely animals," "the stars," "lakes, forests, ocean," "the beautiful trees," "everything he created," and "the earth in general."

A rangy, veteran circus worker who had heard about my research walked beside me down a corridor and said he wanted to share something but asked me to make sure I did not let anyone know he shared these thoughts with me. He did not want to get teased for expressing his spiritual ideas. The first thing he told me was that he thought the circus was the best place one could be spiritual, because you had constant opportunities for the corporal works of mercy; caring for people who were in need. Then he went on to share a bit more of his circus experience. He told me that when it is midnight and you are clearing a lot in the rain, it is hard work to load up and get on the road. You get in the truck, bone tired, wet, and covered with mud. You are driving on a dark road looking through the spattered windshield and all of a sudden the clouds part and the moon shines directly before you. At that moment, you just have to know there is a God. For him, he said, the Christian message is illustrated in the wasted mud lot that is empty and dead but the next day is transformed in glory.

Overall, spiritual awareness appears to be a highly developed sense in many circus people. Some will attribute it to the difficulties of their lifestyle and the inherent dangers in the acts being performed.

One woman said, "I am always praying for those in the circus....You have Him (God) in mind easier than when you are at home...When I was performing, you get very nervous, you constantly have Him in mind, "Okay, God, please help me." "Then you do the trick and say, "Thank you, God."

A French woman said, "The relationship between a performer and God is gigantic. It is usually God first and then me."

One young woman shared a mystical experience she had right in the midst of her act. She was high above the crowd performing on the chiffon when she experienced a white light. Her immediate interpretation was that it was a gift from God, the presence of the Holy Spirit. "I felt the light start at the top and come to me." This is an otherwise undramatic person who described her prayer life as different depending on the circumstances of the day. And simply, she says: "At night I pray typically the Our Father, the Hail Mary, and then I tell God the history of the day."

Gratitude marks Tino Wallenda's high wire troupe as well. "We begin each performance by standing in a circle, holding hands and thanking God for allowing us to walk the wire under his protection."[42] Some who have experienced falls or other mishaps have been re-energized in their life of prayer and gratitude as was the woman who said, "After my accident, I thank God for my life and my family." Another woman whose fall resulted in a concussion says, "...now I am sensitive to God."

Living on the edge, often far from home, evokes an awareness of vulnerability and a desire for security. One young woman told me, "It was easier at home because I was surrounded by Christians. Now I'm alone, faced with trials. I pray all the time and all day long."

Acceptance of ultimate dependence on the divine, turning to the embrace of a loving God, is a common, although not universal, response to the unique character of life in the circus.

Tino Wallenda, who has been performing in various acts since he was two years old, gives his understanding of this in an image from his own family. When he carries one of his children on his shoulders across the wire, people frequently ask if they are afraid. The answer is "No....Because that's my father." "As they have confidence in me, I have confidence in my heavenly Father. I know that He will take me all the way across the chasm of life until I meet Him face to face."[43]

Christians believe that the closest they can come to a true image of God is in Jesus, the itinerant preacher. Jesus taught, as he wandered from place to place, that God is intimate. God's reign is within us. The temple cannot hold God and yet the temple is meant as a house of prayer, for all to be able to pray. God is for all and with all. Awareness of God's presence is itself access to the divine reality which makes every part of the landscape a potentially sacred space.

In or out of the circus world, when a worker enters an office each morning and opens the Bible to read a passage before

---

42 Tino Wallenda. *Walking the Straight and Narrow: Lessons in Faith from the High Wire*, (Gainesville, FL: Bridge-Logos, 2005)106.

43 Tino Wallenda. *Walking the Straight and Narrow: Lessons in Faith from the High Wire*, (Gainesville, FL: Bridge-Logos, 2005) xi.

turning on the computer, God's grace is invoked on all that will happen in that small arena throughout the day. Any single spot on earth, no matter how small nor insignificant in the scope of world realities, can be a place to embrace the divine love who embraces all that is.

Robert Lax portrays the circus tent itself as a sacred space, a tent like that which held God's presence in the wilderness, and from which the chosen ministers reached out to God's people. But, the people are within this tent and the ministers proceed to them through the performance entrance, the archway between the ordinary and the sublime. Certainly the circus tent rising over a hard packed dirt lot transforms that dreary spot into a terrain of grace and beauty. With flags flying on high it draws many into its precincts to experience a new dimension of life.

Within the circus, there are certain culturally agreed on centers of sacred space, particularly each person's moveable home and also the center ring which is set apart for performances. There are temporarily created sacred spaces, designated as such by the desire of those present to turn their hearts and minds toward God. So what was formerly, and will be again soon, a storage space, a stairway, or a cookhouse, is consecrated as holy for this moment of grace.

Father John O'Brien, a long-time friend and much-loved spiritual director, told how he often had people tell him that they didn't have to go to church to pray. John would agree with them since certainly God is everywhere. However, he would always go on to the challenge, "When was the last time you actually took a half-hour to pray? Where do you actually pray? How often?" But this would be a somewhat difficult question for a circus person to answer. Prayer may be frequent but the place and time vary with the demands of the day.

Until the Missionaries of the Sacred Heart found a new rhythm of prayer in the circus life, they too found it difficult to continue their deeply ingrained formal religious practices. Annual retreat weeks continued to be a source of spiritual nourishment but daily prayer structures needed to be adapted. Early on, Sister Dorothy explained, "One of the hardest things about this life if that there's very little time for contemplative prayer. You need at least an hour at a time for that....And it's not often that we have a solid hour to devote to that."[44]

Gradually their prayer styles evolved into a more flexible constellation of sacred Liturgy whenever possible, conversational prayer throughout the day, and concentrated efforts to identify occasional longer periods of time for extended prayer.

Many circus people know and respect the value of a concrete time and place to pray with other believers. However, when that is not possible, they walk their talk and find territories and times to encounter the ever-present holy Beloved. With a diametrically opposed lifestyle of constant movement as compared to treasured stability, spiritual circus folks incorporate the monks' pursuit of a fusion between prayer and work.

In the monastic life, the ideal is to allow prayer to suffuse all work so that one is constantly aware of the Divine presence. This is the desire of many who embrace the circus lifestyle as well. They seek to undertake all that they do in communion with God, whether that work is performed in the center ring or behind the scenes. Sister Bernard, a Missionary of the Sacred Heart, ascribes to this attitude. When asked about finding room for prayer in her circus life, according to a newspaper interview, she said, "'I've learned to be very flexible.' Her motto: 'Make work your prayer.'"[45]

For all believers, every space has the potential to be sacred space. The cosmic reality continues in existence by the loving power of God, the creative source and sustenance of all that is. Every atom of the world is filled to overflowing with God's abiding presence. In God, we "live and move and have our being." Consecrating portions of the universe to help connect to the divine is a spiritual practice appropriate for application not just to permanent structures but to every nook and cranny where we seek to turn to God. "Look! God's dwelling place is now among the people, and God will dwell with them. They will be God's people, and God will be with them and be their God." (Revelations 21:3)

---

44 Susan De Matteo. "Circus nuns juggle demands, challenges in unusual ministry," *Catholic East Texas*, (November 15, 2002) 5.
45 Claudia McDonnell. "Three-Ring Vocation," *Catholic New York*, (April 2004) 41.

Creator God spread out a tent over the cosmos. One of the rings spinning within the greater universe, the earth, filled with delights, revolves. A host of performers parade the spectacular, glittering and bold with beauty. The whole is sustained as a sacred circle in which we each take our turns, blooming flowers, splashing sea creatures, and generation after generation of graced children of God.

Everywhere within the blessed circle, the orb of earth, is holy ground, and holy breath, and full gift of grace. We turn and bow before the One who rejoices in the presentation. The heavenly host, "witnesses in a great cloud on every side of us," (Hebrews 12:1) the communion of angels and saints in whose midst we perform, cheers us on.

CHAPTER 3

God is on the Journey Not Only at the Destination

"I have not dwelt in a house from the day I brought Israel up out of Egypt to this day. I have moved from one tent site to another, from one dwelling place to another."
(1 Chronicles 17:5)

It is time to move on to the next location. Everything is put away and tied down in the house trailers. Bikes and satellite dishes are brought in and those trailers pulled by trucks get hitched up. The jump to the new town begins. In some trailers, the ride begins with prayer for safe journey and thanksgiving for having a job in these difficult days. For others, religious music accompanies the travelers on radio or on CD's. Families use this time together in close proximity to talk about God and God's ways.

In one small train compartment, a group of young women crowd together with joyful fervor and join in their weekly Bible study. As the wheels turn on truck, or trailer, or train, the continual pilgrims watch the changing face of nature and wonder at God's greatness. They praise God's beauty reflected in mountain, lake, and fertile field.

In society outside the circus, motion phrases are often used to describe contemporary life. We are on the move, going places, in a hurry to get somewhere, living in the fast lane, or running on empty. At the same time life is often compared to a journey, the length of our life a kind of road we traverse from beginning to end. Journey is also one of the most common images for spiritual life. Words like road, path, pilgrimage, and walk pepper the language of spiritual development.

However, it is rare that we actually feel the kind of movement this image suggests. Most of us live in substantial dwellings for long periods of time and remain rather settled. This makes it difficult sometimes to absorb the reality that we "have here no lasting dwelling." (Hebrews 13:14)

The illusory permanence of our homes can keep us from preparing for the day when the physical house of the body will be "like a shepherd's tent...pulled down and taken from me," (Isaiah 38:12) that time when our "tent threads will be cut." (Job 4:21). In other translations the message is the same, for all of us there will be a time when each one can say my "tent is pulled up and thrown away" and "like a shepherd's tent my house has been pulled down and taken from me."

Circus people, on the other hand, experience the daily or weekly physical uprooting that makes the image of being on a passage through time a more concrete expression. Many hours on the road on a regular basis engenders complicated emotional responses among those who endure the toil of such travel, yet thrill to the excitement of movement, seeing varying parts of the country, and starting fresh over and over.

In the midst of explaining that the circus lifestyle has a great attraction for her and her spouse, one sixty-three-year old woman working in a mud circus told me about her seventy-five-year old husband's last jump to a new location. "We both enjoy it. It doesn't make sense. He drives that big white truck over there, a big semi. Going into the last town we had two-hundred-fifty-eight miles. He left at one in the morning and got in at seven in the morning. Traffic was terrible."

The ambivalent feeling about travel may be common but the choice to remain on the road is often seen as being a blessing more than as a curse. One sixty-five year old man explained,

"I have loved the circus since I saw my first one at age five. When I retired from a thirty-one year teaching career at age fifty-five, I immediately joined a circus. I like the travel, the people who are in the circus, and the nomadic lifestyle."

Circus people are tent people. Even their homes resemble tents in that they must be portable, either individually or as part of a mobile caravan. Similar to the nomadic tribes found in the book of Genesis, they fold up their 'tents' when it is time to move to a new location. They are like Abraham, Sarah, and their extended family who "journeyed from one stopping place to the next. (Gen. 13:1-3)." [46]

Circus people, however, travel in semis, rv's, trailers, or the more glamorous sounding but tightly confined quarters of a circus train but they still must carry everything they need with them. They batten down the hatches before they set off on a new leg of their journey. If they are in trailers, they hitch up to their trucks. They search out dump stations to get rid of their waste and hope that electricity and water is turned on at the new site so that they can drag their hoses and cords to the hook ups. When they arrive at the lot, they go through the intricate maneuvers necessary to park their vehicles in a tight pattern to use the space provided in an efficient manner, then depending on their vehicle, they may need to level the trailer, connect lines and hoses to electricity and water, and set up house again, taking needed items out of locked storage spaces.

Their itinerant lives are not focused on a homestead since they carry their homes with them. They live in temporary structures that move with them. They work in actual tents that are put up and taken down on a regular basis. Circus people are not seeking a particular destination but take their talents and offer them to each community along the route.[47]

The architecture of their lives reflects the flexible nature of their dwellings. Circus minister, Little Sister Jo, told me, "The road teaches you a certain spirituality." Home sweet home is on the road

---

46 Kees Waaijman. *Spirituality: Forms, Foundations, Methods*, trans. John Vriend, (Leuven: Peeters, 2002) 63.
47 All of this is very similar to a major theme in Genesis 12-50, that of nomadic travel. "Itinerary accounts (not to be confused with travel stories which have a starting point and a terminus) describe the migratory movements of seminomadic communities."Kees Waaijman. *Spirituality: Forms, Foundations, Methods*, trans. John Vriend, (Leuven: Peeters, 2002) 62-63.

and God is understood as being with circus people on their journey not waiting for them only at their destination. They are nomads and pilgrims, visible symbols of the metaphors we frequently use to describe our lived reality in time.

One seventh-generation circus family member's saga illustrates the type of international journey many circus folks make. She was born in North Africa and she traveled from Portugal to New York as part of the first European act Ringling brought over after World War II. But Portugal was not where she and her relatives began their lives. In her words, "My sister and I were born in Algiers. My brother was born in Oslo, Norway. My sister was born in Mexico City. My cousin was born in Budapest, Hungary, and I am married to a Spaniard from Madrid." Right now she is especially happy that her children were born in the United States and are now the eighth generation of the family in circus life.

A twenty-seven year old woman who was born in the circus told me, "Actually I was born in a trailer, in an RV. So, I've been all my life in the circus."

People who live and work in the circus choose a migratory existence. Their common farewell to those in the circus or not is, "See you down the road." In community with one another they journey from place to place to bring their performance to others along their path. Especially in rural areas, they make the show available for those who cannot travel to other types of entertainment which are at a distance from their homes.[48] For those in mud circuses in particular, this means working in all kinds of conditions, rain, sleet, occasional snow, and the consequent mud.

This is a life considered far from ordinary and yet it is followed by people whose spiritual desires resonate with many who do not share their lifestyle. Having God as companion on the journey is epitomized by, though certainly not limited to, circus people. Many would resonate with the woman who spoke of God in this way, "He is my guide, my confidante in all difficulties and joys," and the man who said, "I do not know if it is conversing, nor do I have time to

---

48 One of the towns regularly visited by the Roberts Brothers Circus, known for having a strong commitment to family life, was recognized with a plaque for bringing the circus to sparsely populated areas in Maine.

pray formally, but I feel as though I am accompanied by Him." In a 2007 Christmas letter, the Little Sisters referred to God not only as companion on the way but as "the One who is our road."

Travel is a major part of their life. And it is one of the most valued aspects of circus life. Despite the repetition of the show and the routine of set up, and break down, the movement from place to place keeps circus life from being boring. When asked what life is like, statements such as "Never the same," and "Everyday is unique. There are not two days the same," were common responses. Waking up in one town and going to sleep in another guarantees variety.

The comic side of constantly being on the move comes through in a story captured in the MSC Journal. One of the circus women asked a gas attendant about a particular exit. "The attendant asked, "Where are you going?"

Dotty: "I can't remember."

Attendant: "Where are you coming from?"

Dotty: I forget but it is 50 miles away and the name of the place is in my trunk!"[49]

The overall attitude toward the travel leans toward the positive despite the inconveniences it entails. It speaks of adventure, of hope. A retired circus worker said, "The thrill of a new town added to the everyday shows." Another said, "Everybody in the circus feels that tomorrow is always going to be a better day. It's going to be a nicer lot....So, it's like you're always looking forward to the next step." Sister Dorothy records an overheard conversation that supports this attitude. "The day after the blow down one of the circus people was asked, "How are things?" Reply: "Very good, thank you." "But wasn't there a blow down?" "Oh, yes, but that was yesterday." That is part of the circus philosophy. Yesterday was yesterday. We are today."[50]

Circus people are a migrant community of people who consider it important to travel with God. Several of those interviewed spoke

---
49 Sr. Dorothy Fabritze, *MSC Circus Journal*, (Quitman, Georgia, March 9, 2000).
50 *Sister Dorothy Fabritze.* MSC Circus Journal, (La Grange, Georgia, March 21, 2000).

of praying every time they start out on the road. They pray for safety. They pray just to be in God's presence. They embrace the nomadic life, not focused on homestead but carrying their homes with them. One woman explained that the main spiritual practice she uses to keep close to God is learning to appreciate what is available each day wherever she finds herself. She works at being aware of the blessings that each milieu of her constant travel makes possible. Remarking on the shady trees and small pond she found on a morning stroll, she remarked, "If I was home, we live just outside of Philadelphia, Pa, I wouldn't come here for the day but because I am here I try to enjoy what this place has to offer."

Life in the circus is life on the move. Circus members are not seeking a particular destination at the end of a long journey but take their talents and offer them to each community along the road. They travel on an annual circuit moving from place to place across many states in a single season. They move as a unit with an advance person preceding them, placing arrows to point the way along the route and making arrangements for their arrival in the next town.

In contrast to the elaborate costumes and drama of their performances, circus people live a physically simple life. It is not as detached as Jesus who "had no place to lay his head." But with even the most generous portable space possible, what one can carry is limited and this in itself determines that people live simply in regard to material goods. There are weight restrictions for trucks and trailers on many roads and bridges. There are space constrictions for everyone. And what one can and cannot bring into one's circus train compartment is strictly limited. Consumerism would be hard to sustain under these circumstances.[51]

One unmarried dancer in her early 20's lives on the train and told me that the lifestyle which does not allow the accumulation

---

51 Provided as a benefit for employees who do not have their own portable housing, the Ringling Brothers' trains carry equipment and transport animals as well as people. There are stringent regulations on how long the train can travel before stopping to exercise and tend to the animals onboard. The train, with over 35 coach cars plus flatbeds and other rail cars, extends one mile along the track. As several residents have told me, it can be quite difficult to visit friends because of the long walk to their compartment. Train compartments vary from single narrow units to half car family living spaces, depending on one's role in the circus. The tiniest units are the size of cells no hermit would envy. There is also a strict discipline of cleanliness on the train to insure that no vermin join the tour. One woman religious thought her early convent room was larger and the life less restrictive than that required of those living on the train.

excess goods was helpful for her because it allows her to save money for when she moves on from the circus life.[52] Despite the glamour evident in the ring, backstage life is generally quiet as well as uncluttered.

Outside entertainment is also limited by the demanding schedule. Younger performers and workers without families go into town to explore the local night life after the last show, especially in big cities. A few folks may wander to a nearby casino late at night and others look for a nearby tavern. But, the majority of folks go back to their living quarters after the last show to get some rest before the next day's activities begin all over again. Some folks use down time or riding time in creative ways such as writing poetry or doing crafts like needlework, knitting, crocheting, quilting, and creating hooked rugs, usually as gifts.

Computers are becoming increasingly popular and some folks mentioned playing video games in off hours. However, computers can only be used for internet communication when there is wireless access since constant movement precludes cable or phone line connections. When connections are available, some people use their computers to chat with other people.

There are no clubs or organizations holding meetings that must be attended. There are no sports leagues for adults or children. There is no way to borrow books from the library since one will not be back in town for one or two years at the earliest. The lack of excessive distractions and the over stimulation common in other realms of contemporary life may help circus folks focus more clearly on God's presence in their everyday lives.

The migrant life of the circus fortifies the conviction that God is on the journey not primarily at a given destination or hoped for end point. Their home is on the road. The presence of God is primarily experienced in everyday life. One woman commented, "The presence of the Lord is always with you."

There is no Sabbath time in a circus. God's touch may be sensed in a more intense dimension in certain special celebrations

---

52 Dancers in the large circuses often intend to stay for a limited time and then leave circus life. Unless they develop other skills, there are not many small circuses which hire people solely as dancers.

but it is neither dependent on nor relegated to those moments of formal worship. The call is to find God where one is, not wait until the conditions are ideal for communion with God.

Sister Dorothy, one of the Missionaries of the Sacred Heart who works in the circus, describes how this form of life has reshaped her own prayer practices. "'I used to have a monastic spirituality. I had scheduled time for work and for prayer.' Now ... she has a 'spirituality of the working world" ... and finds that she can pray 'in the middle of anywhere.'"[53]

A forty-seven year old woman said, "We are just people with unusual jobs. The traveling schedule keeps us from attending services, but I believe God is with us wherever we go."

In this study, forty-one percent of those questioned responded to an open ended question on whether they pray and how often by saying "All the time" or "Constantly." Another forty-seven percent indicated that they pray often or frequently. Sixty-four percent said that they also spend at least some time reading their sacred scriptures. One person mentioned that the Bible is in a special place in her house. A young woman discusses the Scripture "with my mom on the phone." A fifty year-old man reported, "I read the Bible before I go to bed, two pages every night. When I finish the Bible, I begin again. I have done this since my accident in 1995." Others talk about reading the Scriptures when they have problems. Some read some passages on their own everyday and some read the Bible in the company of other believers.

The train compartment Scripture Study group mentioned above consists mainly of young dancers from various countries in South America. They meet weekly in a nineteen- year old Brazilian woman's train compartment for Bible reflection and sharing. One twenty-seven year old participant said, "We read the Scriptures and try to transfer the messages for our reality." For some the love of Scripture preceded their arrival in the circus. One young woman recalls being nervous when she was hired and was leaving home for the first time. She opened the Bible and read the words which she translates into English as, "Do not be discouraged. God will be with you wherever you go."

---

53   Claudia McDonnell "Three-Ring Vocation," *Catholic New York*, (April 2004) 41.

Group Bible sharing is sometimes hindered by language restraints. One group from various countries with more than one language used Spanish as a common language. Some of them met an interested young woman who only spoke English but they invited her to join them and said they would figure out how to take care of the language differences. However in another circus Bible group, a thirty-one year old woman who only spoke Spanish was told that if she could speak English she would be able to join their group, but otherwise they did not know how to work it out.

When asked whether she ever reads her Scriptures, a twenty-eight year old Muslim woman instantly produced the pocket-sized Arabic Qur'an that she and her husband read throughout the day when they have a few moments to themselves, "in the bus, walking, when done work, and in between." Ribbons marked both of their places and she revealed that she had read the full text at least three times through.

A similar-aged young man, however, responded differently. "No. For Muslims you have to have a special mindset to read it. Your mind has to be clear. I have no time."

Several people mentioned Bible Study groups sponsored by one or the other family or individual in a house trailer. A middle-aged Christian woman regretted that her current circus did not have a Scripture group. "In the other circus, every Friday one member has a Bible study. We go the whole year. It's nice. You get to learn....But they don't have that here."

Another woman who is trying to read the Bible everyday remarked on having enjoyed her subscription to "The Daily Word," a periodical booklet which offers insights into Scripture. Some mention other prayer books which supplement their Scripture reading.

Prayer, Scripture reading, and religious formation happen in diverse situations in circus life. I have observed one of the Sisters conducting Religious Education classes on a relocated car seat in the back of an equipment truck. Later as she listened for her cues to open and close the curtain, she handed out small sheets of paper with Bible verses handwritten on them the night before for those who had requested this special service. For two years Sister Dorothy was part of the Prop Crew and handled the heavy curtain 100 times a show allowing animals and performers into and back from the ring. This provided opportune moments to talk informally with many circus folks. "They knew that I would be there, and they would just come over and in the darkened area just talk to me about whatever they wanted to talk, and wonderful things happened. Wonderful spiritual things happened, just because I was there."[54]

Religious Education sessions take place in other places as well, for example, on staircases, in empty storage rooms, and in the tent when practice and performances are not taking place. One woman said that she talks to her children about God's ways while they are on the road, "usually in the car going somewhere because they can't jump out. The radio is off and they can still tune me out but they know I'm talking about events in a spiritual way or I'm praying."

A number of circus people told me that they spend some of their time listening to religious music and/or praying during each jump while driving from place to place. A fifty-seven year old man wrote, "I play worship music on the radio and listen to somebody preach on the radio. Prayer is the number one priority for every believer. If you don't pray, you don't have a relationship with God. Prayer is communicating with God. No communication, no relationship, no real life with God."

There are many stressful situations in circus life as elsewhere. Some of the negatives mentioned are the bad opinion some people have of circus people even though they are primarily families, difficulties dealing with animal rights' protests and gas prices. In their challenging moments – vehicle breakdowns,[55] trying to find a place to do laundry, figuring out how to shop, where to get help when in physical or mental distress – God is the one reality they can count on to be ever present.

---

54 Rich Phillips. "This family DOES live in a circus." www.cnn.com/2009/LIVING/wayoflife/01/25/circus.family.life/index.html, (January 27, 2009).
55 Vehicle breakdowns are a constant concern. Owners tease the last drop of life out of their respective equipment trucks and the trailers in which they live. Some circus groups travel in a kind of convoy to make sure if there is a breakdown that someone else will be able to lend a hand. If a breakdown requires repairs, some alternate transportation has to be used and then the drivers need to find a way to return whatever distance has been traveled to pick up the vehicle and join up with the rest of the group.

In an article on migrant spirituality, Maria Frascati Lochhead writes, "The journey of a migrant is never just geographical but also spiritual....The individual takes a spiritual journey that parallels the physical one. God becomes the one constant."[56]

God provides the still center of their stability. God is where their home is. God is more than a symbol of solidity in the midst of change but in some ways this attitude toward God reminds me of a physical sign which comforted a military family's children. This woman, not involved in the circus but still familiar with frequent relocation, told me of her youth when her father's assignments caused the inevitable moves associated with army life. She shared how her mother helped them all to feel rooted wherever they settled. Her tradition was that when they relocated, the first thing to be unpacked was a large cooking pot in which the mom cooked their favorite dishes. Once the children saw that pot, they knew they were home.

In a similar fashion, for circus people, no matter the terrain they travel nor where they set up their shelter for the night or for the week, God is there. When they turn to God, they know that they are home.

Kees Waaijman recounts a similar pattern formalized by the ancients in faith in a ritual of arrival at a new grazing ground. There were three steps in this process, 1) pitching the tent, 2) setting up a stone as altar, and 3) calling out the name Yahweh. "This calling "out" (or "in")was an act of making God present....This is the original meaning of the name YHWH..."Let him be present. May he let his face shine upon us. May he assert his power here."[57]

Calling on the presence of God is not such a formal process as that provided in the stories of Genesis. It is a more common and frequent part of everyday life. They seem to echo in their lives the sentiments of the Little Flower, Therese of Lisieux: "For me, prayer is a surge of the heart; it is a simple look toward heaven, it is a cry of recognition and of love, embracing both trial and joy."[58] That

---

56   Maria Frascati Lochhead. "Being at the edge: Retracing he spiritual journey of the migrant to God and self," *Migration World Magazine*, (Staten Island, 1999) Vol. 27, Iss. 4; p. 18.
57   Kees Waaijman. *Spirituality: Forms, Foundations, Methods.* trans. John Vriend, (Leuven: Peeters, 2002) 63-64.
58   St. Therese of Lisieux, Manuscrits autobiographiques, C25r, cited by the *Catechism of the Catholic Church*, 2558.

turning to God for circus folks takes many forms but for those who are centered in the divine presence, prayer is their breath of life. The instantaneous, spontaneous nature of responses to questions about prayer from young and old, men and women alike, amazed me more than almost any other aspect of the interview process in this study.

The wisdom on prayer held by the circus people is best expressed in their own words.

"I think circus folks pray more than almost anybody. It's natural."

"You pray, pray a lot. You talk and you know very well he is listening.'

"I talk to God like he's standing right there, my best friend in the whole world. I can hide nothing. God knows everything. I just know that he's there. It is a rough life."

"I talk …to say thanks not just because I need something…. When I can't sleep at night, I pray to Papa God…When I am out and other people are afraid…I say to the people, Papa God is with us, don't worry – trust in Papa God."

"Sometimes it is very easy to talk to God – other times it is hard to still my mind and to be quiet. Sometimes I just don't want to talk to God. Thankfully, no matter how I may feel, He is always with me and I hope He understands."

"I pray all the time. The last thing before I go to bed, thanks – and the first thing when I get up – Help."[59]

"I am thinking of God 100% of my waking day. As a Muslim, I say, "Of the name of God" before everything: before eating, working, etc."

"I pray 5 times a day, in the morning, at noon, 4, 7, and 9. I asked a Professional when I was in Morocco because I used to cry

---

[59] Prayer before going to bed, on waking, before the performance, and when traveling were specified quite frequently in the completed surveys. A number also mentioned grace before meals, prayer to recognize the good even in bad things that happen during the day, and prayer for spiritual growth.

when I couldn't do it at the proper times. He said it was okay. It is only not good if you don't pray. When I am working I can't do it at the exact time. I talk to Allah and say that I can't do it at the same time....He helps me. I am very happy."

"I have silent prayer whenever I sit down."

"I am big on good energy. After a prayer to God (I pray to God or Goddess), I have two times as much energy."

A thirty year old woman reported that in her household they pray, "When we eat and when we finish eating. Sometimes we are so hungry, we eat and then we thank God."

Some circus people have specific devotions that support their prayer life. Jesus' mother, Mary, was mentioned as an important part of several members' spiritual life. She was referred to as the Madonna, the Virgin Mother, Our Lady of Guadalupe, and Our Lady of Fatima.

During a presentation in Sarasota, Florida, Aurelia Nock, retired member of a multi-generational circus family, shared several spiritual dreams she has experienced, dreams which have included encounters with the Madonna as one who gave her comfort and encouragement.

A young woman explained her relationship to Jesus' mother: "I pray for Mary to stay by my side because she was a strong woman and I want to be strong."

A formal Islamic practice supports the faith of some Muslim believers who work in the circus. One young Muslim woman explained to me that she keeps the Ramadan Fast each year, refraining from food and drink from six in the morning until six at night, while maintaining her full work schedule.[60]

A fifty-one year old woman stated a special practice she uses to remind her of God's presence. Her simple technique is taking some time each day to recognize "all the God-incidences in my life."

---

60 Since Ramadan goes from sun-up to sun-down, the fast can be extremely difficult in some parts of the world. One Moroccan Muslim told of only three hours of darkness in which to eat while the circus was in Alaska at a time of year when the light shone for twenty-one hours each day.

For their part, the Sisters maintain the practice of an annual retreat which they negotiate for in their contracts. A centering space in their labyrinthine journey, retreat time provides a still point in their path across a broad landscape. It is a time to savor the wisdom gleaned wending round a generous harvest field. Besides this respite and in addition to daily prayer in their chapel and the community religious services in which they are involved, both communities of religious women serving in the circus have used State and National Parks as places of prayer and quiet meditation when possible. One of the Sisters in circus ministry said: "For me prayer is a relationship I live. I reserve some special times to nurture and savor this relationship each day, each week, but, at the same time, I feel in constant dialogue, even if it doesn't involve words. This is the precious dimension of my life that gives me meaning and confidence and 'fire.' "

In the comic strip "Family Circus, little Billy is often sent on errands but never takes a direct route. He wanders far and wide exploring mud puddles, contemplating a snail's passage, and picking up sticks along the way. Eventually he returns home having completed his assigned task. His circuitous route, however, was obviously much more about being aware of and enjoying the world around him then about finishing a particular assignment. For him, the journey is always more than the way to a destination.

The journey of a circus troupe is also much more than the completion of an annual circuit for those who migrate from place to place throughout the season. It is about connecting with those with whom they share their life. It is about reaching out to bring happiness to others. It is about appreciating the journey.

What can we learn about God from those who go from place to place without a permanent destination, and yet seek the face of God? These travelers are not on a traditional pilgrimage, to a specific site on the map. Therefore their search for the divine source of life is an inner journey, as is that of all spiritual seekers. In Christian theology, God is not rooted in a selected space, neither is Church which is the people of God who gather. Church is never merely those structures in which believers come together in God's name. Nor is faithful service to God and others or any other moral behavior circumscribed within any geographical locale. In all of our movements we are within the tent of God's presence.

This was the experience of the nomadic ancestors in faith of the Jewish, Christian, and Muslim communities. They moved frequently and this meant literally pulling up their stakes. "In these departures God took the initiative (Gen. 12:1) and provided assistance to his faithful: "I will be with you ('ehye) and keep you wherever you go…" (Gen. 28:15)."[61]

Robert Wuthnow has summarized the majority of recent trends in spirituality as directed by seekers rather than settlers, focused on images of journey rather than of place.[62] Influential feminist theologian and civil rights activist, Nelle Morton, experienced that shift in direction first hand from the 1950's onward. The story of her transformation is, in fact, titled *The Journey Is Home*.[63]

In the circus world, this type of spirituality has deep roots. Notably, one of the dimensions of travel, both physical and spiritual, which is highlighted by circus life, is that a journey is not always towards something. To be alive is to be changing, moving, journeying, but a proposed destination is far less significant than the way one relates to one's companions along the way and the service one offers to those with whom one's pathways cross.

The journey that is home for the people of the circus is a circle. The circular path is actually a series of cycles, movements out and back, for service and for centering. It includes traveling with one's circus companions for long stretches of time and returning to home base to spend precious time alone with one's most intimate friends and family members. Then the direction shifts toward packing up and setting out again with a new constellation of circus companions. All of this proceeds so that the company of roving entertainers can perform for the many people they relate to in audience after audience. The show people keep those who come to watch enthralled but they leave them behind as the next audience draws them forward. The load out begins again and the nomadic community continues its rounds.

---

61 Kees Waaijman. *Spirituality: Forms, Foundations, Methods*, trans. John Vriend, (Leuven: Peeters, 2002) 63-64.
62 Robert Wuthnow. *After Heaven: Spiritualities in America Since the 1950's*, (Berkeley: University of California Press, 1998).
63 Nelle Morton. *The Journey is Home*, (Boston: Beacon Press, 1985).

In the non-circus environment, life's journey has many similarities. Many of us spend a good deal of time in cars or public transportation moving from one place to another. We go out and do our act, sometimes jumping through many hoops, in service to the larger community. We can be doing this as volunteers or we can be working for our livelihood. In the process we join with companions who have the same mission at this moment and in this place. Between times we return to those to whom we are most closely bound by bonds of family and friendship. We spend time together, repair our physical and psychic equipment, restock our spiritual supplies, review our performance, and then set out again to repeat the cycle.

One compelling message from the circus example of being at home with God on the journey is that one should not wait but use the time one has right now. Do not wait until one can make that desired retreat or take that day off. Realizing that God is available right here and right now, pray. Pray for five minutes in the bank line. Talk to God during the traffic jam. Practice the presence of God. And as any juggler will tell you, practice means repeated efforts, working on the muscle memory, the physical and mental focus that becomes a natural motion, an almost automatic habit. Spiritual practice requires that type of repetition and focus as well until the awareness of the presence of God mimics the unconscious act of breathing in and out.

We turn our hearts toward the divine. Even when mind and body move across diverse terrain, we can breathe in the life of God, the holiness of God's Spirit, which is within us, and among us, and always beyond us, embracing us in our whole sphere of existence wherever we are. "Lord, you have been our dwelling place throughout all generations." (Psalm 90:1)

No straight line journey, this circuit of ours across the years. Our mortal homes cross back and forth, Capernaum to Jerusalem, and then back through Capernaum again. Loading in as we arrive at each new site, we stay in places more or less hospitable along life's route. And if blessed to travel with those of common hope and vision, we circle up to pray as one small cell of faith before we take our place approaching each new performance.

Meeting old friends along familiar routes, we offer our gifts at each arena or vacant lot to new acquaintances as well. Behind us remains a sprinkling of joy and hope shimmering in hearts open to wonder, now rejoicing anew on their own journeys. All of us now ready to load out and move on, intersecting circles of life, attempting to carry forward shared peace, good news.

On the road, we follow the signs that point the way forward. Jesus, sojourner on earth, has traveled the road before us. He has completed the earthly route from life through death to new life in glory. Much like the circus 24-hour advance person who precedes and marks the circus route, Jesus the Christ has gone before us on this journey of human existence. Having traversed the path before us, our leader knows the terrain. Jesus is in fact the Way we want to follow. Disciples, we look for the indications, like circus route arrows, that point us toward our desired destination. Led by the Spirit, we seek God's signs in every age and circumstance, in Word and world of wonder. We follow the wisdom directions provided for us, not tacked on wood or metal posts, but written in our hearts. Not as aimless wanderers but as disciples guided by a living Spirit we press forward in confidence.

Companion God, not left behind nor waiting at the coming stop, travels the route with nomads. No new decision this, but a pattern known from desert days with Abraham, Sarah, and Hagar, Moses, Miriam, and Aaron. The presence always there to those who know how to name the pillars of cloud and fire in their midst.

CHAPTER 4

Identity is not Captured by a Task or Title

"Enlarge the place of your tent, stretch you tent curtains wide, do not hold back; lengthen your cords, strengthen your stakes." (Isaiah 54:2)

It is eleven p.m. in Circus Chimera. A nimble young man scampers across the top of the tent, detaches the top flag, and unfastens the hooks attaching the tent to the center pole, and starts rolling up the tent to dismantle the circus before it moves to the next town. Just a half hour before the same young man hung in a tight-fitting costume, upside down on a horizontal bar suspended from the underside of that same high canopy. Head hanging down and feet to the ceiling, he had swung first one foot and then the other into subway straps attached across the metal support. After several other daring feats, he adroitly descended and stood glowing in the adulation of the crowd, taking bows for this amazing performance with a huge grin. But the center ring was just one locus of this skilled star's work for the evening. Helping to dismantle the tent for the move to the next town in New Mexico, was another, and it was done with just as much alacrity and élan.

Speaking with a motorcyclist who had earlier in the day driven in death defying circles around a large circular metal cage called ominously the "Globe of Death," I asked what he planned to do in the following year. "Well, I'd like to get another job doing motorcycle work," he said in a thoughtful way, "but, if not, I'll probably sell concessions." One year this adventurous young man will race within a metal globe during one thrilling part of the daily show. In the next year he may play his part in the circus ensemble in a less dramatic way by selling souvenirs and refreshments.

Not much later, I met the woman managing the wardrobe, supervising the process of caring for the costumes used in each show, washing, sewing, re-heeling dancing shoes, and keeping everything in order for the performers. With no sign of regret, she told me that she had been a featured aerialist for many years but decided it was time to stop performing and take a job backstage instead.

A dog-trainer working in another circus mentioned that she had left an executive position with a six-figure annual income several years before. Her chosen change of occupation gives her great joy in rescuing abandoned dogs and performing with her beloved pets as part of the circus community.

In the circus, a widely acknowledged but not always lived universal truth is in high profile, what one does is not who that person is or the sum of his or her gifts. We are more than our chosen or assigned roles in life.

This recognition begins with the realization that it is almost impossible to tell what background those not born into the circus life have come from. The man who has become head elephant trainer worked as a cosmetologist and hairdresser. Ringling's first featured female vocalist graduated high school at 16, studied botany in college, and later worked in musical theater before she joined the circus. The long-time booking agent spent many prior years in the CIA after he received his Ph.D. in political science. Others have come from corporate careers or from no special career at all. Laborers, teachers, the unemployed, accountants, and mechanics, all funnel into the big top to work together. Where they have been is insignificant. Who they are and what they are able to contribute to the project at hand, this is what counts. A willingness to do what needs to be done for the success of the show is paramount.

Circus members need to have a concern for the overall project and not just their current part in bringing the show to life. Especially in mud shows, the smaller circuses which move most frequently, most people have more than one job to do. One retired woman related her experience, "We were all expected to contribute equally in loading, performing, tear down.... No prima donnas."

This team effort in mud shows is particularly in evidence when a storm approaches the lot. Everyone pitches in to tear down the tent and dismantle the midway attractions. Strong winds have the ability to cause a blow down, when the tent collapses. This can have disastrous effects and everybody has a stake in protecting one another and the show. After her first experience of one such emergency response, Sister Dorothy wrote, "I observed that ALL helped during the storm. As a family we eat, move, provide a show, clean up, and work together in emergencies. We are the Body of Christ – living, being, celebrating, suffering together."[64]

Even though many jobs are assigned to particular individuals, there is always more that needs to be done than can fit into the regular job descriptions. In some cases, temporary help joins up in one town or another but in most cases, the regulars need to fill in the gaps. The juggling performer may get some "cherry pie," extra pay, for helping to clear the lot before moving onto the next location. The clown may be out in front of the tent to greet patrons as they arrive and sell coloring books before and after the show and during intermission. The company's cook might leave the cook tent to sell balloons before and after the performance. Some veterans delight in referring to the years when their primary job was being GU. That title means Generally Useful and has the evident significance of being able to do whatever needs to be done whenever it needs to be completed.

For those who have spent their lives in the circus, learning as many skills as one can is part of the fabric of life. Aurelia Nock, member of a one-hundred-sixty-year circus family tradition, tells of her childhood performance doing the *pas de deux* on horseback. To give her act more flare, she wanted a longer tutu. Her family's response was to tell her that she had to learn how to make costumes, and she did. The overall attitude toward various kinds of work is captured in a saying her grandmother, a circus owner, would often use, "The one who cleans the street is as important as the one who wears a hat."

---

64   Sister Dorothy Fabritze. *MSC Circus Journal*, (Douglas, Georgia: March 11, 2000).

The need to be able to do some tasks is partially related to the amount of time spent on the road. In an interview, one older woman explained, "You learn to be a mechanic. I have changed pistons on my car. There is no time and no money to do it in a shop with one day stands and doing two shows."

The tempo of circus responsibility is more like that of a folk dance rather than a forced march. As in the traditional Hora or other circle dance, the community makes a series of circular maneuvers in which one person or one couple at a time may move into the center and be the focus of everyone's attention. After a time, as the music continues, the circle widens to welcome back those at the center, and another takes center stage.

The rhythm of circus life is of the whole life, which includes the performance but is not limited to those moments alone. There is a calmness borne of the routine repetition of the grandest of acts. Two young people chat about the most ordinary realities, then one breaks off the conversation for a while, enters the ring with a gleaming smile set in a confident show face, makes the sign of the cross, and deftly climbs a 30 foot sway pole as if it were a simple staircase. After amazing the crowds with feats of daring bravado and skill, he takes his bows and descends. A quick change, and then a return to his companion who makes a comment on the performance and picks up the conversation so recently suspended. It is the same person who lives behind the scenes and who dazzles during the show. This may be difficult for those in the audience to grasp but it is what everyone who shares the circus life comprehends. They know each other as persons, with virtues and vanities, strengths and secrets, fears and fantasies. Their relationships are with the full persons with whom they share their lives. Each person's identity includes his/her contribution to the common effort but no one's personhood is limited to that one aspect. Within the community individuals are judged by who they are not only what they can do.

When it is no longer possible or desirable to continue in one role in the circus, it is common for folks to move onto other areas of responsibility. The aerialist who made her own costumes early in her career feels comfortable in the wardrobe department because she knows what needs to be done. The boss clown and dog trainer in one circus spoke easily of his former days in the seemingly more prestigious role of circus owner. His expression said that it was the life he loved, not the particular position he had in the company. One Russian acrobat came to the United States to perform. He then went on to work with the electricians, found a way to take formal courses to become certified, and is now head electrician.

The circus as a whole is everyone's job. Members multi-task on a regular basis and are not defined by just one area of endeavor. It is expected that one's gifts will be used for the whole community's endeavor not only to enhance oneself. This intermixing of roles can have the effect of grounding individuals and keeping them from identifying themselves with their roles. It also makes it easier to relate to each other without inserting status considerations into relationships, at least for some people. One former small circus member explained that they, "…just did not have the luxury of harboring a grudge. We all had to work together to make the show a success. The trombonist climbed in the rafters to rig the trapeze. The Spanish Web team would make dinner. The band leader would drive the truck, etc."

There are some headliners who choose to live more aloofly. In small circuses they may be treated differently by getting a food allowance instead of eating the common meal of the other workers. In large circuses, the stars may have their own dressing area. One male star performer when asked about things in the circus that might make it difficult to stay close to God said, "Like all things around us there are temptations. One that may be greater in the circus is the temptation to pride. That could mount up. Other than that, nothing different than life in the world outside."[65]

And yet, even if some star attractions of the show do choose a bit of isolation outside the ring, they still rely on many others for their effectiveness and safety. Paid more than some other workers, they are not more secure. They still have limited contracts, one or two years at the most, with a need always to be developing new acts. Tino Wallenda after talking about the strength and flexibility training that is essential for performers, refers also to their constant

---

65 In her memoir, Victoria Cristiani Rossi recounts an instance of healing forgiveness after jealousy had divided her famous family. "The Lord, in all his mercy, had performed a true miracle of reconciliation, saving us all from the fatal undertow of pride." Victoria Rossi. <u>Spangles, Elephants, Violets and Me: The Circus Inside Out</u>, (New York: iUniverse, 2007) 238.

need to come up with creative new approaches. The attitude he puts forth is, "Whatever you did in your past, good for you. But it's what you're doing now that really counts."[66]

Obviously when one has the ability to draw all eyes in an arena to oneself there is a sense of satisfaction. Becoming the focal point of awe for all those in the stands, receiving the adulation of the crowd at the fulfillment of a difficult feat can also have a somewhat addictive effect; lead to an inflated sense of self-importance.

The whole purpose of the circus is to bring delight and awe to an audience and everyone in the troupe is meant to share in the sense of accomplishment which arises when those in attendance express their delight. The temptation comes when an individual begins to believe that he or she is the unique pivotal force of the whole company's success.

Regularly becoming involved in the less dramatic tasks that go into a production, being aware first hand of what it really takes to make one's shining moment possible can help balance the ego trip lying in wait for the gifted artists who are the visible center of attention day after day and night after night. When it is time to move into another role, the connections to others whose supportive roles one has come to value, eases the transition from performer into teacher, or wardrobe keeper, or assistant in some other area in need of personnel. It may be a temporary or permanent realignment of roles but one can maintain inner peace in contributing to the success of the circus community's total project of opening others' hearts to joy and wonder.

On a personal level, dating and marriage between performers and non-performers is very common. On a professional level, the most noticeable attitude among the vast majority of performers is an awareness of their dependence and interdependence rather than their relative performance status.

In the Introduction to his book, "Walking the Straight and Narrow: Lessons in Faith from the High Wire," Tino Wallenda whose ancestry includes acrobats, jugglers, clowns, flying trapeze artists, and animal trainers as well as the famed cadre of high wire

---

[66] Tino Wallenda. *Walking the Straight and Narrow: Lessons in Faith from the High Wire*, (Gainesville, FL: Bridge-Logos, 2005) 124.

performers, writes, "Some people think that because my family is famous that I am somehow special. I'm not....the name Wallenda is well known in the circus world, but we've tried not to exploit the name for monetary gain or our own benefit. We've always tried to excel and do our best for God."[67]

Some people miss the center ring when they can no longer perform. A young woman who was pregnant and working in the nursery temporarily felt an urge to join others in practicing her act on the chiffons. She resisted but made it clear that she couldn't wait to work on the show again. Another woman expressed her preference for performing as well but from a different perspective. Referring to her family's decision to sell the circus they owned, she commented, "It is better to be a performer than an owner – less worries."

And yet, there is a limit to the number of years in which one can perform in some of the particularly grueling acts. The physical demands make it a blessing to have something else to move onto when it is time to make a change, especially when that something else is seen as critical to the total project as well.[68]

Overall the circus world is a unique community, a kind of family of families. It is a remarkable system of distinct individuals and family units who live an intimately connected village-style life in the midst of a larger, more complex society. Because of their continual movement across long distances across the country, their intersection with the general population is tangential to their more insulated communal circus interactions. Although travel gives them the opportunity to have friends and acquaintances visit them at the circus on their route across the country, these relationships do not seem to have the same binding strength as the intra-circus ties do. There seem to be relatively few deep, long-term relationships with individuals outside the circle of extended family and those who share the circus life.

---

67 Tino Wallenda. *Walking the Straight and Narrow: Lessons in Faith from the High Wire*, (Gainesville, FL: Bridge-Logos, 2005) xiii.
68 Sometimes, changing circumstances lead folks to move from one type of show to an entirely different one. A roustabout nicknamed 'cowboy' explained that he had come to the circus at the request of his family. They were concerned about the number of injuries he has sustained in his prior work performing on the rodeo circuit. So he switched to a different type of traveling entertainment, the circus.

For true circus folks, not necessarily for temporary hires, their identity is wrapped most tightly to the common bonds of circus life as a whole then it is to any specific role within that nomadic tribe. They are bound to each other by a quest to continue the deeply rooted tradition of circus as a traveling band of performers. As a coordinated troupe they work to bring thrilling entertainment to audiences wherever they stop along the road. As one young woman phrased it: "Circus is an attitude of service. You have to work together as a team, even if you don't like all your teammates. They are my brother or sister."

What are some characteristics of spirituality which may be expressed in but are not tied to a specific job or role which one takes on in daily life? Without defining spirituality, there are identifiable attributes of those described as spiritual which will paint a helpful picture.

The spiritual person is directed from within, is connected to God, and values others. The spiritual person is one with the universe and is aware of dimensions beyond the physical, sensitive to deeper realities. The holy person loves God and the things of God, is dedicated to prayer and the service of others for love's sake. This person refers experiences back to God as their source and responds to God's promptings from within and from without, especially in relationships with others. The spiritual person has moral values that govern his or her actions, values that are captured in the Golden Rule. This person acts according to the Spirit of God and the fruits of the Spirit, "love, joy, peace, patience, kindness, goodness, faithfulness, gentleness and self-control" (Galatians 5:22-23) are evident in her or his life. The spiritual person is hungry to be with others who share the same sentiments and is strengthened by being with those who have similar values.

Christians maintain that spiritual life needs a body, a locus, a community. Religion binds you to others pursuing the same path of awareness of and fidelity to the Divine. The skeleton that provides the structural ground for the spiritual life of the Catholic Christian community is made of Scripture and Tradition. There is a living text and a living history of meaning. But, as the Acts of the Apostles confirms, the Spirit cannot be restrained by an external identity of belongingness. Many may receive the outpouring of the

Identity is not Captured by a Task or Title

Spirit, without yet being part of a formal communion of faith. (see Acts 10:44-48) Their true identity is revealed in the love they show for others.

Looking from another perspective, those most deeply imbedded in the community's structure have their own challenges, much like the star performers in the circus. Leadership figures can be tempted to view themselves as the most essential components of the group and may isolate themselves. They know and often proclaim the ideal of the importance of every member and the ideal of discipleship in a community of equals. In black and white in printed form this is a simpler accomplishment than it is in flesh and blood reality. Members in leadership positions in religious congregations, high level employees in corporations, and directors of volunteer endeavors alike can become somewhat dysfunctional when assigned to new roles which they have come to view as inferior to their earlier positions. With a loss of status and power, their sense of identity suffers. They continue to expect the same type of relationship with others that their prior roles required. They have gotten used to deferential treatment and general acceptance of their decisions. Inadvertently they have come to experience themselves being at the pinnacle of a pyramid model which they might intellectually reject. In their mind's eye they believe in the equal value of all members of the community but when they lose direct influence, there is a sting of loss and sometimes a depression that may lead to difficulty in adjusting to a new role.

Perhaps circus life can show how frequent involvement in various levels of responsibility for the common project, even when one is functioning in a high profile position, can keep the vision of servant leadership more clearly in view. Paul's commentary on the importance of the foot and the hand as well as the eyes to the body's full flourishing can be experienced in the flesh.

Those is publicly acknowledged leadership roles are not the only folks who face these types of challenges. Retirement or having one's children move into adulthood can disturb the core sense of identity of those facing these transitions. The question arises, "Who am I when I no longer have this role?" Trying different activities, exploring new ways to contribute to what one considers important projects in life, even while working and/or parenting full time may make the question easier to resolve when the time comes to make a change. Expanding one's sense of self beyond one's circumscribed current set of relationships may free one to take on fresh roles at various stages in life with peace of heart and continued self-satisfaction.

According to Robert Greenleaf who has brought the term servant leadership into common consciousness, servant leaders in every dimension of life are those who in any setting always seek out what needs to be done and do it. They acknowledge that their identity is deeply enmeshed in a communal reality. They realize that personal happiness follows upon corporate success not mere individual accomplishment. Circus folks who take on the care of the whole with limited regard to the status of the work required exemplify these essential elements of effective servant leadership.

CHAPTER 5

Interdependence is Grace and Responsibility

"Paul went to visit them (Aquila and Priscilla), and when he found they were tentmakers, of the same trade as himself, he lodged with them, and they worked together." (Acts 18:3)

The large metal sphere called "The Globe of Death" is rolled into the ring. Everything is arranged and then the performers' father and some of his other sons make a final check. One by one, they inspect the chains holding the equipment in place. The lights come on; the motorcycles roar into the tent and throughout the act, the father and brothers of those circling inside, hold onto the chains and keep a watchful eye until the riders complete their dangerous circuits.

The Swiss star of the show has become pregnant. Neither she nor her Mexican fiancé know much about finding medical care on the road. Their American performing friend takes on the task. He researches clinics in the towns to which they will travel, calls ahead and makes appointments, and drives them in his vehicle to visit the doctor in between shows.

A rare dark day arrives. There are no performances. It is a chance to get some rest, catch up on laundry or other chores, soak in a bubble bath, or tour the local sites. I ask my friends how they will spend the day. They say that they plan to join a van load of those planning to visit another circus in a neighboring town. They will have a few brief moments to see circus folk working there and then they will join the audience and watch the show.

A similar event occurs when I go to the circus which has set up near my town. As I take my seat, I notice the clowns in the performance ring give a nod to someone in the stands. When I turn in that direction, Barry Lubin who performs as one of the most celebrated clowns in the circus world is sitting next to me. On his day off, this inductee into the International Clown Hall of Fame, who takes on the persona of 'Grandma' in his act, has taken the time to enjoy the performance given by other members of the circus community.

An almost universally accepted sign of spiritual strength, particularly in the Christian tradition, is the bond of love. According to Edith Wyschogrod in *Saints and Post*-modernism, "saintly life is defined as one in which compassion for the Other, irrespective of cost to the saint, is the primary trait."[69] Holiness, not necessarily of the canonized variety, exhibits itself in the circus particularly in the community bonds and mutual ministry expressed by those who care for one another. One woman in the circus talked about the close community gathered there: "It is a different family but still caring and giving."

Jesus' Gospel imperative to "Love one another as I have loved you," (John 15:12) is the most challenging of spiritual demands. But the First Letter of John affirms the command with this clarification, "For anyone who does not love his brother [or sister], whom he has seen, cannot love God, whom he has not seen." (1 John 4:20) Relationships within the circus community can be viewed against the backdrop of the expectation of a spirit of love in community. However, even those community bonds which exist without an overt reference to faith are sacred ties. For Christians, they point to the relational self-revelation of God as love, vitally present in all encounters of self-giving love.

A middle-aged circus worker said it simply, "By doing good to others you are following your religion...I think that is also a

---

69 Edith Wyschogrod. *Saints and Post-Modernism: Revisioning Moral Philosophy*, (Chicago: University of Chicago Press, 1990) xxiii.

good way to stay close to God." Another said, "I don't pray much but am always helping people one way or another." A thirty-two year old said, "Ultimately God is love. So, if I treat you with love, then that is being God. Not being God, you know…keeping God in the center of my life. I always have to live in love."

At least one person saw communion with others not only as a means of serving in love but also as a source of grace for herself, "When I am not able to read the Bible, I am able to look at people and be reminded of how God is in us all or where God needs to be."

Some of the most common phrases survey respondents used to express the way their faith affects their actions include: accepting of those who come from different backgrounds, forgiving, patient, kind, sensitive to others' needs, responsive, fair and compassionate to those who are poor or less fortunate, tolerant of difficulties, expecting the best of others, reaching out to others, trying to understand people, being honest, and treating others "as if they were family." One young woman described some of her prayer requests: "I ask God to stay with me, to be with me so I can follow His path, to use me to do good things, to be good with everybody, to be patient when I am tired. During the day, be my eyes, be my mind, to help me pass good things to others." A twenty-seven year old said, "I can see God in my friends. They are my family here when my real family is so far away."

Mutual support is at the heart of circus life. People in the circus world have strong relationships of care for one another. This does not mean every single person gets along with each other person. One woman mentioned that she takes these concerns to prayer. "I make little requests to help me…to be nice to other people, when angry with others…I pray for that." Another woman, thirty-years old wrote, "I pray for peace. I pray for people who don't like me." A younger woman remarked that she tries to remember, "Biting my tongue is not the weak think to do, even if it seems to be."

Obviously within the close quarters of the circus, there are the expected preferences for some and distance from others. However, overall there is a communion within the body which is marked and strong. There is a shared experience that fashions ties which remain more significant than petty irritations or differences of opinion.

Compared to life in the surrounding community during the winter break, a young woman wrote, "In my everyday life off the road you are too busy with little things. On the road you don't even turn the TV on because we all do things together."

In their first Winter Quarters, before they set out on the circus route, the MSC Sisters were invited to stay with the owner's family. By that evening, Sister Bernard sat beside the owner sewing slippers for two performers while Sister Dorothy and the owner's husband filled the trucks with gas and prepared for the first leg of their journey. At the conclusion of the community journal for that evening, Sister Dorothy exclaimed, "The circus is truly a FAMILY."[70]

The ties that bind in a circus last beyond the time one remains in that world. A long-time circus worker left and moved into the business world for a number of years. When she retired she went to Sarasota and said it felt like she was coming home to family because she knew so many of the people who lived there. She does not remember the names of the important people she worked with in business but she said, "I do remember the circus people." Some circus people who own homes near the winter quarters make arrangements for others who live year round in trailers to set up in the backyard area of the house.

A thirty-one-year old, seventh-generation circus member wrote, "I love the closeness of everyone and the way we help and work together. …I'm in it because I love it."

The wife in one older couple who works the circus only in summers had this to say: "You feel like it's an extended family. Everybody watches out for you, much more than in our neighborhood….We're going home next Saturday, and I'm sure the neighbors will see the truck pull up but nobody would ever come out and say, "Hi, how are you doing?" On the circus everybody looks out for their neighbor."

This couple followed a common pattern in smaller circuses, where several trailers make an effort to park near each other in every new lot. In an interview in a different circus, a single man reported, "Usually in small tent shows you all park the same way,

---

[70] Sister Dorothy Fabritze. *MSC Circus Journal*, (March 5, 2000).

so you always have the same neighbors. It's just the way it usually works out." Those small groups form even closer bonds with each other and interact more frequently.[71]

Another woman, a thirty-four year old, who was staying home for the summer for the first time, echoed the older couple's experience. "I believe that faith and spirituality are easier to live on the road....Most of the people on the road are religious and those who are not are usually good people at heart. There seems to be more of a distance from Christian life in many of the people I interact with at home on a daily basis."

Brent DeWitt, who started many years ago as a seven-year old apprentice in the circus appreciates the small town nature of the mud circus. He told a newspaper reporter, "That's what the circus is – a little city that moves. Nothing changes but the grass."[72]

In the work aspects of the little town atmosphere of its traveling community, all members of a circus are strikingly interdependent. If a stagehand tightens each required component of a performer's apparatus, the entertainer can succeed. If not, he or she may easily fall or be injured during the act. If concessionaires do not sell enough of their wares, a decrease in profits can lead to a reduction in employees or the close of the circus. If the "twenty-four hour man," the person who precedes the circus by a day to post directional arrows for the caravan and make sure that everything is ready at the next site, does a good job, the circus will arrive in time and be able to erect the tent and the midway before the audience arrives. If not, everyone suffers.[73]

Aerialists depend on the riggers.[74] The dancers depend on the wardrobe folks to have their costumes ready for their quick changes during the performance, to re-secure their well worn heels

---

71 One performer who used to be with a small circus experiencing such an intimate living situation, felt lonely when he moved to Ringling. He kept his own trailer but most performers lived on the train and he hadn't yet bonded with the others living in RV's.
72 "Maintaining tradition: Old-fashioned circus makes stop in Troutman," *Record and Landmark*, (Statesville, NC: April 6, 2000). 4A.
73 A couple who work as a 24-hour team traveling ahead of the show has this schedule: "We get up at 5 a.m. and help park vehicles as they arrive on the lot. Eat breakfast. Wife gives school children tour of animals and circus vehicles...husband discusses route with manager. 10 a.m. leaves to put up arrows. Come back, pick up trailer, get lunch from cookhouse (to eat on the road). Check facilities for the next day's show, find hay, water ...Eat dinner. Go to bed at 10 p.m."
74 Sometimes a performer who does particularly precarious work will ask a trusted rigger to go with him or her on a circuit.

and launder their sequined outfits in between shows. The person drawing the curtain to allow acts to enter and exit depends on cues from the production manager. The production only succeeds when everyone does his or her part for the good of everyone else.[75]

The insular nature of life on the move creates a special common reality peculiar to those who live in it together. One clown said, "It is an extreme lifestyle, like being in a war. There is a deep bond because of an intense shared experience."

Living within a compact area insures that the community life of circus members extends beyond show-related activities. House trailers are parked side by side with barely six feet between them. One survey respondent said, "On any lot it doesn't take too long to find somebody, if you know what they live in. We don't go by street numbers or house numbers. We go by (RV) brand names." Those who do not have personal or family motor homes have tiny living quarters on trains or in truck cabs or trailers.

One twenty-eight-year old expressed the isolation her small living space created for her when she first joined the circus: "At first it was no good, one room for me and my husband. I don't like the small room. There are different people. I was all alone and didn't know anyone. With time, now it is okay. Now it is changed. I have friends and talk to people."

Some workers in mud circuses have even less personal space. They share undivided sleeping space in the back of the tractor trailers used to haul equipment from one location to the next.

In these close quarters, the people of the circus carve out interpersonal relationships, family life, and community connections. Much of the casual, friendly interaction and the inevitable small town type gossip sharing between circus workers takes place in public spaces in or around the tent or arena, the equipment areas, or the common eating areas. Ringling Brothers has a set of weights set up backstage to help the performers and other members of the

---

75 Due to the heavy dependence of the show on every member of the community, there are hefty fines on mud circuses for anyone who comes in drunk and more than one incident can lead to instant dismissal. Larger circuses with union contracts can have addiction services as part of their health care plan but being impaired on the job is not tolerated.

company to keep in good physical shape. In between shows, those using the equipment and those waiting their turn share friendly banter. Others chat as they stake out a spot on the floor beside equipment boxes to boot up their computers. A quick pick up game of soccer on the lot between shows can also provide some friendly interaction for players and spectators alike.

In many circuses the clowns have a special bond even within the troupe's community. The backstage area where clowns take on the greasepaint and costumes which define their personas is called "clown alley." One member of the group told me that clowns form "a community, supporting each other."

Smaller circuses frequently have a cook tent open to all as a benefit of their employment. Although there is not much time for lingering, table companionship still exerts its own power to draw people together into a community of conversation.

Sixteen percent of the survey respondents singled out living in close community with co-workers and family as features of circus life which make it easier to live a spiritual life.

According to one sixty-eight year old woman, "The close community and need to depend on one another, I think, helps one stay close to God. One often meets God in our interactions with other people and we certainly have the opportunity as we travel and share our lives with the circus community." A sixty-five year old man responded to a question about what about circus life helps him stay close to God by saying, "The 'family' I have acquired by being in the circus. I have met so many wonderful people who are believers."

A few people had an opposite opinion. These individuals find it more challenging to stay spiritual because of the close quarters which they share with others. According to one young woman, "Faith helps but it is difficult to be so close. We live together, work together, and travel together. Sometimes you get tired of each other. It's like being in a pressure cooker. Constant irritation grates you. You hope you turn out to be a pearl." The closeness is an opportunity for self-improvement according to one woman. "I tend to look for the best in people. The circus life gave me a chance to practice what I believe. Faith grows with exercise."

Despite the potential and real irritations among those living closely together on the circus, a long time circus member told me the unity is greater than any divisions. They might argue among themselves, she said, but when anything is against the circus as a whole, they forget the interpersonal feuds and stick together. A special phrase for this attitude is used widely in circus circles. True circus folks understand what it means to be "With It and For It."

The smaller community of those who live and work in the circus is much more intimate than the passing community they form with the audience at each performance. They appreciate the audience and seek to not only entertain but to treat those who come to the show with kindness and respect.[76] The big tent is the place where they welcome one and all, where they perform their repeated ritual acts of awesome feats, but it is not their home. The show arena is not where they live and sleep and talk with family and friends.

Because so much of their lives are public, their home spaces are treated with great respect. Perhaps because of the very density of their living arrangements, mechanisms are in place to safeguard personal time and space. New members soon become aware of the tacit agreement that one visits only by invitation. In general, to respect one another's limited privacy, people do not just stop by to see one another. The Midway or some other shared space is the place people usually meet. Then if one wants to have the other over for a visit he or she takes the guest home personally. Occasionally someone will test the boundaries by repeatedly finding reasons to walk by another's trailer in the hopes of being invited in but there it seems there is no animosity if the hint is not taken.

The Sisters' trailer is occasionally the site of small group social gatherings. From time to time they invite a few of those with whom they work to come over for breakfast or an afternoon snack. In the case of the Missionary Sisters of the Sacred Heart, Sr. Bernard Overkamp is a professional cook and this is an especially alluring invitation. Over German pancakes, or eggs and bacon with homemade bread, those who gather share conversation,

---

[76] At least one ticket seller, however, said that dealing with the public can be a strain. She said, "You try to be nice....You try in this business to remember that it's old hat to us but for the people coming to the circus it's not."

concerns, and plans for the future. Sr. Bernard's bread is greatly appreciated and sometimes, when she has the time and energy, she bakes a few extra loaves as gifts to share with others.

The web of relationships in a circus is drawn with as much complexity as any other social network. Individual friendships overlap with small groups of compatible companions, and inevitably, the romantic intimacies of couples. Though they live close to one another, the busy schedule means couples have to squeeze precious moments together whenever they can. One worker described how he finished his work with the elephants after the show and then would "...go to concessions to help my girlfriend pack up her supplies, then go to the train together." One man discussed the difficulties which accompany a heavy work schedule. "It can be very hard on relationships. You have to work hard to create a balance." And one person who has been unsuccessful in developing a permanent relationship in the circus remarked, "It is better with a family. If you come on the circus as a family already, it is easier…. A marriage is a nuclear community and it's a support. When one person gets down, the other builds them up, back and forth, and that's how you keep your heads above water." The young woman who wrote the following would agree. She responded to a question about what in circus helps her live a spiritual life by saying, "My husband helps with everything. His loving me helps me love others."

Circus community ties, however, extend beyond the circle of one's current company. Although leaving the show can be painful because one is leaving day to day life within a unique community, present companions do not sever their ties completely. Circus people frequently move from one circus to another. Contracts are limited to one or two years at most; shows change. In fact, all during the current season, performers and those hoping to become performers, are trying out fresh routines, and developing more challenging skills with an eye toward the coming year. New shows, new circuses, new acts, these all lead to new relationships. The choice of which circus to apply to when one's contract expires, can be motivated by many forces. One seeks to be with family or friends in another circus, or to leave behind differences with management in one's current circus, or to pursue an exciting opportunity which has opened up somewhere else.

But the relationships that have been formed in a prior circus remain alive and continue to exert a pull toward those who are now in different circuses. They want to visit other circus people, even if they get almost no time to socialize with their counterparts. Some of this is due to close family connections in the broader circus world where it may appear that everybody is related to everybody in the circus.

However, with or without relatives nearby, as one of the opening descriptions indicated, it is not uncommon for folks to find a way to visit each other if two circuses are set up in towns of relatively close proximity. If one of the circuses in question has a dark day or only one show, a number of people will spend their precious free time traveling together to see the other circus. There may be some professional enthusiasm in the visit, a desire to see what the other circuses are doing this year. But that is not the main rationale for their visit. It is to see circus friends they have spent time with along the way. They express their support by their presence. The sacrifice made is evident but irrelevant, swallowed up by the almost tangible bond which draws them together. Because they are always on the road, circus folks cannot form attachments to the people in the towns they visit. Other circus folks are their primary relationships.

When visiting is not possible, phone calls and email communication sustain relationships. And in the small town atmosphere, news of major events spreads quickly in any given unit about common friends in other circuses.

Circus folks look out for each other. A circus owner asked one of the Sisters to stay behind when a worker was taken into custody for a minor offense. He paid her to stay nearby the jail when the circus moved on so that she could visit the man in prison until his case was decided. Even as the circus moved on to another state, the circus owner was on the phone working for the prisoner's release.

In another situation, one of the circus clowns made it his business to call ahead to towns and cities on the coming schedule to arrange doctor's appointments for a pregnant performer. When traveling in the vicinity of a circus member who is off the road because of an accident, I have seen others make large detours to visit for a brief time. When one electrician suffered spinal cord injuries after an accident, some circus people extended their travel route hundreds of miles between two locations to visit him in New Jersey's Kessler Rehabilitation Center and again when he returned to his family home in Virginia.

When a young woman had blacked out after a fall, her friend sat beside her and sang a song to her. After her recovery, she said, "I felt it was the song of an angel."

Communication problems can become a dividing factor among those who cannot express themselves to one another. One circus owner who expanded his workforce by hiring three deaf laborers quickly realized they could not converse with anyone else. He explored the internet to find a way for the workers to learn sign language. Now they can function more confidently and independently within the community.

And, even when troubles are not the cause, circus people keep close connections. A celebration was the occasion for a festive group to gather in between two performances on one of my visits. One of the wardrobe women was pregnant and close to her due date. Her sister worked on the show, and with the help of others in the wardrobe department, had arranged a baby shower. Worktables were shifted to form a space for food and presents. People had slipped out between shows the day before to come up with gifts for the new baby, both of whose parents were overjoyed at their kindness. Some in costumes, some in dressing robes, some in work clothes, they spent their brief half hour of conviviality enjoying one another's company as if they had all the time in the world. They chatted, ate cake, oohed and aahed at the presents, took some pictures and then dashed back to work.

Sometimes the influence circus folks have on one another is distinctly spiritual. A thirty-nine year old woman described her experience. "When my husband and I first got together we were in a tent circus, Vidbel Old Time Circus. [One of the Vidbels] would talk about God and she would just glow. We got married in her church." Remarking on the overall atmosphere, a seventy-one year old man exclaimed, "The love and connection of all circus people is wonderful. Everyone is one big family."

There are no phone lines on circus lots, but cell phones and other technology, as well as written communication, provide the means for people from various circuses to keep in touch. That mutual interest extends even to those who have moved beyond the circus world either temporarily or permanently. It is a common practice for those who have their own trailers to adjust their travel schedule from one place to another to include a stop for breakfast or another meal with a former circus companion who lives within driving distance of the route. This can be a complicated process involving mapping out new directions, finding a place along the road to meet or a way to meet at someone's home, and anticipating traffic patterns, to make the meeting possible and still insure that the circus folks get to their next site on time.

The Circus Fans Association of America is a national group of people who love the circus and make great efforts to support those who make the circus happen. Founded in 1926, they spread the word about circus world news in their official magazine, *The White Tops*. They also make it a point to visit with the circus troupe when a show is playing near their town. Circus Fans will often make arrangements to meet and go together as a group to a local performance. Those who live and work in the circus enthusiastically anticipate the occasional meals the fans supply as well as some conversation with those they have met year after year on their circuit throughout their regular route.[77]

People who have left the circus world still experience a deep connection to the circus community. They often consider their stay away as only a temporary break and plan to return in the future. On a few visits to the circus I spoke with a former Ringmaster working in the front office and his wife, a performer temporarily working in wardrobe. They were struggling to discern whether God was calling them to leave the circus for awhile and care for his aging parents. Yet, even while we sat chatting over cake and juice, their two little children enthusiastically demonstrated their newly acquired tumbling skills along the narrow trailer's width. It is clear that any departure from the circus world will be a temporary retreat from where their hearts have found their home.

A summer employee at the College of St. Elizabeth, where I teach, happened to see one of the circus photos in my office. He was excited to think that I might have friends in the circus since he

---

[77] The Circus Fans Association of America also has a website (http://www.circusfans.org/) covering circus news and the organization's activities:

had friends in the circus, too. He found out where I was teaching, knocked on my classroom door, and we spent a five-minute conversation talking about the people we know and sharing information on who was in which circus at the moment. He had been in the Ringling Brothers Circus selling concessions, had left for awhile, but told me that he planned to return in the future. As he left with a smile, he took my hand and said, "God bless you." And the blessing was given simply because I knew and cared about some of the people who were sharing life with his circus friends, and by extension with himself. Circus ties are wide and deep.

What about family life? Talking about interdependence necessarily includes an accounting of the most intimate of small communities within the larger circle of circus life. For some families, circus life is passed on from generation to generation. One woman said, "I am a member of a circus family. I'm a part of the fourth generation that has already reached six generations, from 1865 until today." A fifty-seven year old man explained, "It's a family heritage for the most part and I grew up in the business, so I am what I am." In my study, 29% of the respondents were born in the circus and continue in it because it is where they grew up and feel most at home. For other families, it is not considered a permanent situation.

For the multi-generational families, youngsters often begin to perform or work in the circus in some way at a very young age. They learn a variety of skills. Some families are particularly concerned that the youngsters learn not only how to perform but how to present themselves gracefully as well. One sixth-generation mother told of enforcing ballet lessons for her sons, even the one whose ambition was to become a clown. Her three sons are now the seventh-generation of performers, and she says, "God willing, if their sons keep the faith and follow the way, they will be the eighth."[78]

Practice in performing various feats can become a game for circus youngsters. For some of them this takes the shape of a competition with siblings, cousins, and other children. It is the shape of their childhood. However, when they are young adults of eighteen

---

78   The poise developed from learning ballet is often mentioned by performers as an important skill for many circus acts. Equestrian Dorothy Herbert is one performer-author who brings up the topic in reference to horse-riding routines in her memoir: <u>Dorothy Herbert: A Memoir – Riding Sensation of the Age</u>, (Televast, Fl: Dale A. Riker, 2005) 82.

or so, they generally decide if they will continue in circus life or not. Within those families, it is a great source of pride if some members of each new generation choose the circus life. One couple who made sure their children had a good amount of experience in both circus life and a settled life found that "they got mad at us because we exposed them to both things. So, they had to make a choice."

When a circus couple has children, they have to undergo a familiar decision-making process. They have to address such questions as, How can we arrange our lives in such a way that we can be a happy family? How will we provide financially and emotionally for our children's needs? What changes do we need to make in our lifestyle?

Childcare is almost non-existent except in the largest circuses. Either from a desire to be part of the circus, to use one's skills, or to contribute a needed second paycheck to the family, few individuals live as non-working companions of circus workers. Sometimes job responsibilities are rearranged to provide care for the youngsters in a household. Father or mother or both may move from a performance role to office work or some other position that will allow the adults to rotate their presence at home with the children.

All of these decisions are spiritual decisions for a family of faith. The interdependence within the family unit corresponds to the interdependence within the larger circus circumference. God is seen as present in the family unit, giving the gift of relationships and calling for mutual responsibility. Parents seek guidance in making their decisions. They strive to create an environment of love for their children which reflects the love they receive from the Divine Parent, whom one circus mother consistently referred to as Papa God.

Spending a significant amount of time together in travel and on the show site can enhance family bonding. A fifty-seven-year old father in a multi-generational circus family said, "Circus family people are different. Most people are anxious to get their kids out of the home and to college. I am selfish. I want to have my family around. My daughters stay at home until the proper suitor comes. I know it is old-fashioned and might not be other people's way, but it is my way." An older woman discussing her four children and eleven grandchildren remarked, "We are a close family…. They don't sleep over at other people's houses. In the morning all have to practice."

Traveling together offers a unique opportunity for many circus families. It is an extended period of time together in a shared space with time to talk and listen and just be with one another. The long hours on the road can strengthen the bonds of couples and families whose settled time in parking areas is often splintered by runs back and forth to the arena or tent.

The intimate interplay of relationships in a family correspond to the Divine Trinitarian Community of Creator, Redeemer, and Sanctifier in the Christian understanding of God. To be in the image of God is to be called to harmonious, creative interaction within a community of love. Spiritual life in this context is relational life. For families, the closeness of daily life can be a source of communion with the sacred source of life but the intense pressures of that same life can also entail intense pressures. This interdependence at the root of one's coming into existence can lead to fractures as well as to bonding experiences. All relationships are a process of moving toward fullness of life and abundance from the places of pain and partition. Being part of a close-knit larger circus community can provide some relief.

When young people find the person they want to marry, circus life produces some new challenges. If one person is from the circus and one is not, then one of them will be changing his or her lifestyle in a radical way. One woman shared that she was studying law before she met her husband in Mexico. Now they are both working in the circus but, although she likes what she does, she still says, "I am not a circus person." Another woman says she is in the circus, "Because my husband is in the circus. I like to be with him. He doesn't want to go back to Morocco." Still another says, "It's weird. I was supposed to come visit my sister (in the Wardrobe) and I met a guy. When I went back home he wrote and called and I came back and never left."

If both are circus folks, they will need to find a circus in which they can both work at their preferred jobs or one may get a job doing what they prefer and the other may have to find something else to do. If they decide to leave circus life and they are from different countries, they will need to agree on where they want to live.

One of the downsides of a break-up or separation for a couple, is that often, at least for the remainder of a performance season, they have to be in frequent contact and may even have to work with each other on a regular basis. One man going through such a rift felt that the lack of personal time and time to cultivate deep intimate relationships contributed to the break up. He told me how painful it was as he continued to perform with his partner but live separately. And he added, "So, right now I think of God a little bit more than I normally would."

As might seem obvious, marriages between people of different countries are rather common in the circus community which draws its personnel from around the globe. Not everyone in the current study indicated their country of origin, however, among those who did, fifty percent were from the United States, thirty-two percent were from Latin America, twelve percent were from Europe and Russia, and six were from Africa. During my visits to various circuses I have seen a variety of combinations of cultures in many circus families, e.g., couples who are from Mexico and Switzerland, Russia and Spain, Switzerland and Italy, Czechoslovakia and the United States, Algiers and Hungary, the United States and Russia, Russia and Peru, Peru and the United States.

The demands of circus life can make it prohibitive to fulfill the requirements to become legally married. One young couple from Brazil were told they would have to remain in a stable location for a month if they wanted to have a wedding. This, added to the realization that they could not afford the money for a wedding, made them choose to raise their family without getting married. Recently the adult children of these trapeze artists arranged for their delayed marriage with bridal gown and all the trimmings for their parents.

Some of the families with whom I talked believe living in a circus keeps them more closely connected than they would be outside of the circus. Their reasons include the separation from many external distractions and the living quarters which keep them in close and constant contact with one another. The remoteness from some outside influences may allow the family to foster spiritual values with less competition from less appealing alternatives. Living in close quarters can extend the formative realm in which the youngsters can become spiritually mature and the adults are strengthened in their faith. It is a reciprocal reality that a child often can lead an adult to deeper faith as well as the reverse reality.

One mother of eight who married her husband during a winter break said, "There are a lot worse places to raise a child. The small circuses that I speak of are very much like living in a small town where you know everyone and everyone knows you. Also you learn quickly who to avoid and who to make a friend of.... As I look at the world now, I would still rather raise my children on a circus. When we were traveling on the road my children had no access to TV which is probably one of the best things that could have happened to them."

For some families, however, living in such confined circumstances can lead to increased stress in family relationships. One mother spoke of how she used to go outside and pray for help with her children. A priest who worked in the circus noted that, "Marital relations also suffer because of the close living."

Infidelities may not happen at a higher rate than in other settings but the close proximity of everyone's living circumstances makes such digressions difficult to keep secret.

An additional stress on family life is the most common one or two year contract which means that the circus will be creating a new show and performers need to develop fresh acts to try and thrill the audience.[79] One's life remains unsettled until a new job offer is made.

One member of a family may be hired for a particular circus but another may not. If more than one person in a family is hired by different circuses, each with their own unique route, the family may split up for the duration of the year. Husband and wife or parents and their adult children may be on different circuits and see each other only rarely. In other scenarios, one person accepts the offered job and the other will take on a support role so that they can stay together.

In one circus family, both members of a young couple took turns supporting one another. She is Russian and he is from Kansas They both worked as animal handlers. When their new

---

79 Performers can audition for the new shows by interviewing with a current employer, sending a DVD or having potential employers view a website demonstrating the performer's skills, or by participating in annual circus festivals where individuals and groups can demonstrate their abilities. The bigger circuses also have representatives who go out recruiting new talent from around the world.

baby was about to be born, she officially stopped working but, after the birth, he made it clear that he was taking care of the baby. Enthralled with his infant daughter, he claimed the prerogative by asserting that his wife carried the little one for nine months, now it was his turn.

Job security is an important issue for many circus families. A forty-seven year old clown said, "I pray for my children and ask that He gives me the strength so that I can work hard, so that I can support my family."

Financial concerns are the reason many people from other countries choose to come to the United States' circuses. The high unemployment rate in many parts of the world and the low salaries induce many people to leave their families and homelands to earn a living in the circuses in the United States. The families they have left behind continue to exert an important influence in their lives.

The cell phone is a major connection between members of families who are separated from one another. This is a relatively new phenomenon on circuses. In 2000 the MSC Sisters record repeatedly that they had to search out and walk to a phone near the circus lot when they wanted to make a call. But that is no longer the case and, as in the rest of society, cell phones have become a means of constant communication.

A thirty-eight year old performer shared, "There are only me and my husband here. My mom, dad, and daughter are in Russia. Sometimes I talk on the phone about church and especially when sick we ask to pray for each other. My mom cries but I tell her not to worry. I will be alright." This woman, whose daughter is studying in Russia, said she had to say "Thank you" to God for her job because, "I don't have to stay home and just be a housewife and I can make money to help my family…. I send a lot of money home. We have to. We need money for the university."

A woman whose extended family worships together at home misses the experience when she is on the road, so she told me, "Every Monday, I call my sister and ask about the service and how everything went."

One thirty-eight year old woman who reports that she only thinks of God sometimes does, however, think of God "if my mom or daughter calls."

Another whose children are all grown said, "I give them constant reminders. On the phone I always tell them, "Don't despair. Have faith."

A divorced woman said, "My son is with his daddy now. He is Orthodox. When we are together I teach him the sign of the cross and other things. When I talk on the phone with him, we pray together."

A thirty-seven year old woman who is divorced and separated from her child as well said, "I pray to God to bless him. He is the connection when I cannot touch my son. My son is far away. I pray, "Papa God, keep him healthy, safe, okay, happy…In His hands is our future."

A twenty-eight year old woman told me, "I like it when somebody comes and talks to me about God. Most people don't do that. … also I call my family two times a week and talk about God when I talk to them."

Education is a complex task in circus life as are so many otherwise ordinary realities. In large circuses such as the Big Apple Circus and the multiple units of Ringling Brothers Circus, a type of one-room school house is provided by the owners but this is not typical of other circuses. The arena circus type of schooling has certain unique features. School supplies, kept in a large box with fold out shelves, are loaded in and out by the circus crew. Those who teach set them up in whatever back room has been designated as their classroom in each new venue. Once tables are arranged and class has begun, the routine may still be far from normal. Youngsters who are performing in the circus may be answering questions in class one moment, making a dash to be ready for their cue in the next moment. Then they return in costume to rejoin their classmates for the remainder of the day. Most school children, however, are non-performers. Classes are scheduled to coincide with show days, Wednesday through Sunday each week, with travel and load in days as days off from school.

The familiar mantra that parents are the primary educators and faith formation agents of their children is at least as true in the circus world as it is elsewhere. Living in such a close community can provide an extended opportunity for the spiritually formative influence of parents on their children. Initiating children into regular religious rituals which typically are celebrated on Friday, Saturday, or Sunday is a severe challenge. Work and school schedules both make setting aside a traditional sacred Sabbath or prayer day an almost insurmountable challenge.

Mud circuses generally do not provide educational opportunities for school-age youngsters. Some of the options chosen by parents in smaller circuses include correspondence courses, home schooling, or having the children live with extended family either for those months in which the school year and the performance schedule overlap or throughout some entire years. A thirty-year old woman told a little of her story, "I am the fourth generation of a circus family....My parents sent me and my brother and sister to school with my grandfather when he retired, in Guadalajara, Mexico, but I couldn't wait. I was crying every day. We wanted to go back. We missed the show. I like show business. I wanted to be close to Mom and Dad. They teach me and I am still here."

One mother has her children taking correspondence courses but she explained, "I am careful what kind of school he goes to, a Christian school....They pray, sing, and find Bible passages when school starts each day." This was a way for her to get support for sharing her spiritual values with her son while at the same time providing him with a solid education.

Some children go to regular schools during the break between seasons. One family also got involved in religious education during their time off while their children were young. The mother recalled, "When the children were still at home after Mass and after breakfast we would sit around and discuss the day's Gospel. My husband was especially good at this and at one time we both taught catechism classes. In the winter time, of course." Five of her children were also altar servers in their youth.

Other children are sent to boarding schools for some of their schooling. A thirty-nine year old woman said, "Mom and Dad were musicians in the circus. They had six kids. I am the youngest and the only one still in the circus. We went to a Christian school in Montana for awhile. Great memories." Victoria Rossi of the famed Cristiani circus family had a completely different experience. Much of her memoir, *Spangles, Elephants, Violets and Me: The Circus Inside Out*, revolves around painful memories of her time away from the circus while she was in a religious boarding school. Her happiest days were the holidays and vacation months when she returned to life in the circus with her family.[80]

In some cases, one parent will stay behind in the family's winter quarters while the children are of school age. The other parent will go on the road and the whole family will be together during school vacation and in winter quarters.

The Nock family once had an extended indoor performance opportunity. They parked their camper in the woods for the duration. It meant three shows a day, seven days a week rain or shine. But their mother was happy because the children could go to a regular school.

Overall, because of the frequent movement from one circus to another year after year, the educational opportunities and options vary and continuity in a program from year to year can be very difficult. Besides the variances from traditional educational program, in the rapid pace and narrow confines of the circus housing circumstances, there can be a lack of informal educational stimulus for children in some families.

Many life experiences are so different from those in non-circus homes, that there are a number of children who have never seen or assembled a puzzle. On the other hand, the families and circus community provide other intriguing learning opportunities not given to most children. It is part of circus culture that skills are shared. A key element of being in the circus is being in on the secrets, sharing the knowledge of how things are done. There is a desire to communicate that knowledge to those one cares about in the traveling community.

---

80 Victoria Rossi. *Spangles, Elephants, Violets and Me: The Circus Inside Out*, (New York: iUniverse, 2007). She would find out where to meet her parents for the vacation break when they would send her a route card in the mail with the city circled marking where they would be at that time.

Circus skills are passed on from generation to generation and the tiniest youngsters proudly demonstrate amazing skills. Many of the children can juggle and balance and do skillful acrobatic moves that would be the envy of their counterparts outside the circus world. In addition to the enrichment of exposure to many cultures, children also have the opportunity to learn performance skills from a young age.

In one trailer I visited, the seven-year old son practiced juggling while he watched television and talked to his mom about that morning's correspondence course class and what he had learned. A six-year old girl in another circus was receiving ballet lessons from a circus dancer on Fridays before the evening show. In multi-generational performing families, children under five may appear in the ring to bow and complete simple duties and then, well-prepared by their parents, move onto joining fully in the family feats before they reach junior high. The mentoring of young people as well as of other adults is part of the fabric of mutual ministry within the realm of circus life. And young people inevitably rejoice in teaching one another the skills at which they have recently become adept.

The versions of religious formation available to circus children will be discussed in a chapter about ministry. However, the physically close life circus families share together highlights the critical role that the family plays in the children's spiritual formation, no matter what other resources are available. Their insertion within a small working community of remarkable intimacy underlines the opportunities others have to provide role models of a spiritual life lived in close quarters.

The relationship with family and with the circus community is enhanced for circus children with an awareness of their connection to the grandeur of created reality. For those youngsters who are on the road with their parents, there is the opportunity to travel far and wide. They see the scenery of the United States, mighty mountain ranges, richly yielding farmlands, clear lakes, churning rivers, fascinating deserts, and the great variety of towns and cities across their route.

They also have opportunities on occasion to go on field trips in widespread locations throughout the country. The Houston Space Center in Texas, Hershey Park in Pennsylvania, the Smithsonian Institutes in Washington, DC, Sequoia National Park in California, Niagara Falls in New York, and Mount St. Helens in

Washington State can all be part of one season's experience with no additional travel expenses. The enriching opportunities to experience physical and cultural places of beauty and knowledge offer the potential to expand the spiritual awareness of the youngsters who are on the circus journey.

An understanding of many cultures is another positive aspect of the interdependent world of circus life for young people. A clear advantage of being in an international community is that youngsters generally speak several languages. If the parents are of different nationalities, they begin with those two and then gradually add in the languages of the countries in which they perform and those of their friends in the circus. One nine-year old Venezuelan boy lamented that his ten-year old friend, child of a father who was a former Olympian and a mother who was a life-long circus performer, spoke Portuguese, English, Spanish, and Russian, while he only had three of those languages. He enthusiastically said that he intended to pick up the fourth language as soon as possible.

It is not only the children who choose to become multilingual. A seventy-four-year old woman told me "Right now I have five languages. I used to have eight. You meet people from so many countries." And a nineteen-year old who has previously read and discussed the Bible is "currently reading the Bible in Spanish. I'm learning Spanish. It seems more powerful to me in a different language."[81]

In many ways it is a grace and a challenge for all those in the circus living in an international community. The challenge can come from lack of understanding, especially in the larger circuses where three-hundred people may be working closely together. One woman who was not comfortable with companions from other languages and cultures prays for assistance but still says, "Sometimes you wonder if people are talking about you." Clown, Fred Menke, says that humor can help bridge those potential divisions because laughter is the same in any language.

---

81 The knowledge of English among foreign-born circus folks allowed me to interview people from many countries. The only group I was not able to speak with was the young Chinese acrobat troupe in Ringling Brothers' circus. They maintain a close knit and disciplined community within the community with escorts to care for their needs. Members in these troupes are rotated from circus to circus and back to China on a regular basis. Some other circus performers seem to develop a certain affection for the youngsters but extended interpersonal interaction is more difficult to pursue, though some of those from China do take English classes.

For the most part, members freely interact with one another and work side by side regardless of native culture. The folks I have met were from Mexico, Morocco, Algiers, Peru, Spain, Russia, France, the United States, Brazil, Argentina, Colombia, Italy, Austria, Switzerland, Germany, China, Hungary, Poland, Cuba and Nicaragua. Although predominantly Christian, there are also Muslims, Jews, Buddhists, and those with no identifiable belief system. Such a peaceable realm where international diversity is harmonized within a single community is a blessing and perhaps a harbinger of what is possible when many focus on a common positive goal.

Curiosity about others' way of life can lead to rich conversations. A Muslim woman said, "Some people like to ask about the Qur'an when they hear that I can't go to clubs… or dance or go out to drink as a Muslim, they want to know why. I can dance at home but with women only."

Exposure to one another's cultures comes at unexpected moments. Questioning all the hugs being exchanged one day, those from the United States were introduced to the very popular International Women's Day. Obviously celebrated with great fanfare in Europe and other countries, it is somewhat comparable to Mother's Day in the US, but is much broader. Once the information was shared, the American women could be seen congratulating their counterparts from other areas with warm embraces.

An unusual example of the interdependence of some teens from different cultures revolved around preparation for Confirmation. Two young women from Brazil said they wanted to celebrate the sacrament. One of the Sisters agreed to meet with them each week to guide their formation. The only snag is that they spoke Portuguese and Spanish and the Sister did not speak Portuguese and felt that her Spanish was not sufficient for a religious formation process. Two other teens came along and volunteered a solution for the dilemma. They could not speak Portuguese but they could speak Spanish and English and offered their services as translators for the process. To provide the best resources she could Sister asked friends outside the circus to send her Portuguese language Bibles, Missals, and other prayer materials for her candidates. Then the five of them, the four teenagers and Sister, met together weekly for almost a year. During the preparation sessions, she spoke in English, using gestures to supplement her words. The Spanish-speaking

Argentinean teens then translated her stories and instructions into Spanish. The Brazilians would communicate their responses, questions, and reflections in Spanish and their young companions would transmit these back to Sister in English. The final celebration of Confirmation was especially joyous with all those present who had worked to make it possible.

The religious formation of the young people takes place primarily in their families. One father told me that his fourteen-year old daughter wants to learn more about religion now. Up to this point he has focused his attention on the children's moral development, trying to teach them to consider what Jesus would do in certain situations. More than one parent mentioned using a similar methodology, asking in some way for the child to consider what God might think about a certain behavior or action they are considering. This was presented by parents as an effective way to have the children make the right choice.

Only one or two circuses at a time have the possibility of the support of a professional religious educator. Although a few circus people don't stress religion with their young children or teens because they believe that children will get faith only when they are older, most hold religious formation as a very important value. Some believe in God but say they do not talk about it much with their children. However, one baby's mother believes it is never too early and reads a Baby's Bible repetitively to her daughter. "Eventually she'll really know what is going on...." Stating a conviction that this child is truly God's child, she said, "I am the custodian to guide her in the best way I can and not neglect her in any way."

A committed Christian father said, "We have made it a practice to have devotional time together....As a family, we often try to make a habit of having devotion together in the morning before we start the day." Helping children to pray before they go to bed is also a common practice in many families. And a number of parents mentioned that they try to form their children by example and everyday conversations. Mothers and fathers share their beliefs with their children. A forty-seven year old man assured me, "I always tell them that God is first." A twenty-seven year old woman expressed faith sharing as a mutual ministry in her household. "We help each other remembering all the moments that God is with us."

A number of the survey respondents indicated that parents read the Bible or tell Bible stories to their children either before bedtime or at some other time of the day.

On one of Ringling Brothers's websites the following was included in a brief bio of internationally acclaimed daredevil clown, Demetrius Nock, known professionally as Bello. "Bello married his high school sweetheart, Jenny, and has one son, Alex, and two daughters, Amariah and Analiese. Bello feels very strongly about instilling the many morals he has learned from his family and he also influences his children with Bible stories."[82]

This lifelong circus member is passing along the religious faith he has received. He is sharing the gift with his own family. Many of the survey respondents identified the source of their own faith and prayer life in the wisdom they received from their parents and grandparents. Tino Wallenda remembers his grandmother's influence. "She prayed with me, and had great conviction in her faith.... She made God real for us."[83] Many of the parents of circus folks continue to influence their adult children's faith. For example, a thirty-eight year woman confided to me, "My mom sent me Russian Psalms. I read them before I go to bed."

Many of the prayer intentions mentioned by those interviewed included both their own families and the circus family. A thirty-four year old woman said, "Every night I talk with Him. I am grateful for what He has given me. I ask help for my family here and in Mexico, and for the circus people to have a good show." A nineteen year old wrote, "I always say a prayer when I leave, not aloud, for myself, just a simple thank you. Bless my day. Bless my family. My sister is in Iraq, take care of her....My fiancé rides in the globe of death. Every day during the act I think of it extra and pray."

Prayer for one another on a large and small scale can reinforce the deep reality of interconnectedness across borders and religious boundaries as well. One circus woman warned, "It is our fault we make divisions on our roads to God."

---

82   Retrieved from http://www.ringling.com/explore/137/stars/bello.aspx, March,2008. More information about Bello is available on his own website http://www.bellonock.com.
83   Tino Wallenda. *Walking the Straight and Narrow: Lessons in Faith from the High Wire*, (Gainesville, FL: Bridge-Logos, 2005) 18.

Interdependence is Grace and Responsibility

The circus may provide an image of how all people can learn to accept one another within the diverse global community of which we are all a part. In a non-circus world, the simple exercise of considering all the people who make it possible for us to have a loaf of bread and a glass of wine or grape juice as part of an evening meal reveals the widespread connections upon which we all rely. The farmer, the picker, the truck driver, the factory worker, the store manager, and the check out clerk are just a few of the people who, seen or unseen, we need to maintain our strength. We are interdependent components of a multicultural, multi-belief system that comprises our universe. It is clear that what one does affects the rest.

The Church, too, is a large tent including many types of people. The international, inter-faith circus community may help us recognize the grace and responsibility of interdependence within the Big Top of faith, the worldwide household of God. This is a task for all believers. As one woman said, "We are here to help one another, to do God's will. You don't have to wear the clothes of a monk to do God's will." Like the circus, the ecclesial community consists of lawyers and laborers, nurses and nuns, performers and priests, those in the spotlight and those backstage, a great diversity of personalities and opinions and spiritual approaches as well. All members of the Church community are called to find a way to a unity which respects the distinctness of each member, the fulfillment of God's design for God's Reign on this earth, harmonious and peaceful relationships pervading the community of love.

As Sister Dorothy says about the circus, "You have to be very open, because you're constantly dealing with people from different cultures. When you think about it, circus life is just another expression of catholicity, of universality. There's a little bit of everything here, and you have to be ready for it."[84]

The practice of mutual ministry among those in circus life provides a powerful example of the strength to be derived from a common life infused with practical care for one another's needs. Drawn together from many walks of life, gifted with diverse skills, talents, and personalities, the people of the circus share a unifying

---

[84] Susan De Matteo. "Circus nuns juggle demands, challenges in unusual ministry," *Catholic East Texas*, (November 15, 2002).5.

mission and lifestyle. While establishing tacit protocols to respect one another's privacy while living in a constant proximity that could prove grating on the human spirit, they still maintain alertness to one another's needs.

To different degrees within the overlapping circles of their relationships, specific needs activate outreach and support. The more generic human requirement for a sense of belonging and worth is particularly expressed in appreciation of each person's contribution to the success of their shared mission. The burst of joy and beauty emanating from the center ring outward to embrace the audience is celebrated repeatedly within the community of those who most fully understand what that completed production entails.

Each small faith community, whether parish community, family, or community of women or men religious, thrives when mutual ministry undergirds the group's outreach to the broader community. Love within the confines of a more intimate group is frequently more challenging than loving those one works with and for in external ministry. Yet that ministry has the potential to become a grace to those serving and those being served when it arises from a community of practical, everyday care and concern. Personal space and freedom are an integral part of true love in a community of interdependent individuals. There is a rhythm of separation and coming together, a dance of solo and partnered steps. Love orchestrates the melody to sustain a measured movement to and fro.

Mutual ministry is looking out for one another, respecting one another, and valuing the part each person plays in the overall shared project. It is not for the sake of mission, though effective mission thrives in its wake. It is the simple stuff of life that wherever one is, one needs the other. For Christians it is addressed as the relational essence of human life fashioned in the image of God who is eternal mutual communion of Creator, Savior, and Sanctifier.

Every small community of faith in family, parish, or religious congregation, is called to be a community of compassion whose reciprocal loves radiates outward in dedicated service beyond that circle of mutual care. God is love and those who love one another in a committed fashion are sacraments, effective signs, of God's love for those to whom they are sent. The Spirit of Love binds all together; weaves the intricate connections of caring and of need.

CHAPTER 6

Ministry Makes a Difference

"Shouts of joy and victory resound in the tents of the righteous: 'The Lord's right hand has done mighty things!'" (Psalm 118:15)

Two folding chairs sit casually side by side between two travel trailers. Two middle-aged people, a woman and man, lean toward one another in an animated discussion. The Bible on her lap is open and the weekly one-half hour Scripture study is almost over. A quick hug and then he completes putting on his costume and make-up and the clown and the Sister walk toward a tent where she will sell tickets and he will spread infectious smiles throughout the crowd.

It is late evening. The last performance has ended. But, the center ring is not empty. There in the middle is a table covered with a circus print altar cloth. A priest, the national director of circus ministry, presides in matching vestments. Seated in the center ring near the altar are a number of young adults. After a year of preparation in the Rite of Christian Initiation of Adults, they are here to celebrate the Easter Vigil and their Sacraments. The sponsors and the Sister who has been their catechist sit within the ring.[85] This inner circle with its aura of mystery is reserved for those most intimately involved in the sacred rites. Their friends and

---
85 In keeping with the circus tradition, the center ring is kept as a special space set aside for performance. Only those sharing their artistic gifts for the sake of the larger community are to remain within the ring.

family members who have come to share this moment with them are nearby in the stands, praying and singing, and celebrating this holy night of Resurrection under the tent.

Sleepily boarding the early morning shuttle bus from the train to the arena, folks from many lands look up as they hear a cheery hello in the language of their homelands. The German-born Sister who works in the women's wardrobe is already seated greeting one in Chinese, another in Portuguese, a third in Spanish, and the next one in English. Later on some will seek her out for a bit of advice or just another reminder that someone cares.

The beaming mother of a first communicant embraces a Sister, exclaiming, "I never thought my little angel would ever be able to receive First Communion in the circus."

Most circuses have no provision for meeting the religious needs of their personnel. Because of the constant change of location, there can be no stable relationship with a single religious community of worship. There have been a few priests and ministers who have worked with the circus for a few months a year over a period of time but it is a rare occurrence at the present time. The result is that although many of the owners, performers, and other circus workers are obviously deeply religious, they often have had little faith formation.

Exceptions to the lack of formal religious leadership are provided by a few members of two religious communities of women, who support their Sisters engaged in circus ministry on the road. Making a choice that resembles that of earlier worker-priests, these women religious join the circus and are hired to do regular circus jobs in order to be present to and available for others in the circus community. They have traded in the black habits that were the standard attire of women religious in an earlier era for the black shirt and slacks required of those who need to blend into the scenery as they work backstage.

Both the Little Sisters of Jesus and the Missionary Sisters of the Sacred Heart refer to their work as a ministry of presence. At least one woman, who knows both groups well, says that description is insufficient. They also have a ministry of the moment, a flexibility

Ministry Makes a Difference

that allows them to respond to the needs they encounter in their presence to the circus people whose lives they share.

Circus ministry requires employment as a circus worker. Over the years this has meant that the Sisters who minister in the circus have held jobs cooking, repairing costumes, selling balloons and souvenirs, teaching children, helping set up the tent, selling and collecting tickets, opening and closing the curtain during performances, picking up trash left after the circus to make sure the rented lots are left free of debris, and helping in the nursery. This is a far cry from an earlier era of ministry. In fact, I have been told, though I cannot verify this, that in one town in Italy there is still a rule on the books that says that nuns and priests cannot attend the circus, let alone work in one.

So, while many circuses exist without conscious ministers in their midst, there are a few who do. Those who dedicate their service to circus ministry attempt to provide a type of parish life for circus folks. They want the members of the circus family to experience a sense of belonging to the larger Christian community. In the meantime, they almost as a second thought provide a model of living Christian discipleship in the same, sometimes grueling and challenging day-to-day routine as everyone else in circus life.

In only her second journal entry after entering the circus life, Sister Dorothy reflected on a mission-related quotation:

> "Unless people are able to sing their own songs and tell their own stories Christianity will be a foreign import in a foreign packaging, never becoming part of people's own repertoire."[86] These circus people have their stories which they tell. [One man] tells his stories in words, advice, and humor. [His spouse] tells stories in her motherly concern. [Another couple] don't communicate much verbally but the grace, strength and skill of their performance comes from the story of their lives. [A certain clown] speaks his stories in comedy. The tent and prop crew are strong and yet .... [one of them] will leave in May – his wife is expecting a child[87]

---

86 Anthony J. Gittins. *Reading the Clouds: Mission Spirituality for New Times*, (Ligouri, MO: Ligouri Publications, 1999) 66.
87 Sr. Dorothy Fabritze. *MSC Circus Journal*, (Quitman, Georgia, March 9, 2000).

The presence of professional ministers in their midst has the added benefit of tending to enhance the circus community's credibility in the broader community. A typical attitude toward circus people presumes they will live up to a stereotypical bad reputation. However some are willing to rethink that position when they learn that the Sisters are part of the circus. And with that it has the effect of enhancing the self image of circus folks themselves.

It is only those circus folks who have these dedicated servants of God in their community who can know the difference it makes to have a religious presence in their midst. They know the effect it has on the ability to fulfill a variety of spiritual desires for formation and religious celebration They alone also understand the unusual circumstances in which the ministers are working and the limitations within which they have to operate.

Religious activities can only take place in the brief time between shows, practices, travel, and loading the troupe's materials in and out of the performance facilities. An account of some of the experiences of these women may give additional insight into the ways in which the somewhat frenetic circus world can be identified as a sacred space.

Whenever the Sisters are present in a circus they quickly become a hub of religious community for their companions on the journey. None of the Sisters who have traveled with the circus proselytize, set out agendas for what the circus folks need or should do, or even offer any religious outreach unless they are asked by those in the circus. Everyone knows that they are nuns and they work side by side with the other circus employees doing ordinary jobs. They are there for those who need them. Sister Bernard says that she wants to "listen to their stories-to listen with the ears of my heart, to see with the eyes of my heart."[88] They respond to requests and serve as the situation arises. And the requests do come, sometimes slowly, sometimes very rapidly when they join up with a new circus. Sister Dorothy recounts the story of one woman whom she greeted daily without getting a response in return. After more than a year, the woman's first words were, "Sister, can you help me become a Catholic."[89]

---

88 Claudia McDonnell. "Three-Ring Vocation," *Catholic New York*, (April 2004) 40.
89 Barbara Daniels. "Ministry to People on the Move," *MSC Connections*, (Winter 2005) 2.

This deliberate ministry of presence means being there for and with others, and it is deeply appreciated by their companions on the road. One of the circus Sisters wrote, "I would like to accompany the people on their spiritual journey of life. I would like to witness that we, the People of God, are loved by God and that in responding to this love we can live a life of Peace and Joy." They have come to offer spiritual as well as physical companionship to those who live on the road.

A CNN crew captured the comments of some roustabouts who thought that having women religious on the circus would mean that they all had to act pious and walk with their hands folded. They changed their minds in a short space of time and were grateful that they had some women of God with whom they could talk about their concerns. The image of Sr. Dorothy Fabritze pulling the ropes with the others to erect the tent in one scene was followed by a shot of her quiet conversation responding to the private concerns of one of those same men just a few steps away later in the day. The owner of that circus did indicate a decision to set up a cuss jar which received quarter contributions each time someone used swear words around the sisters. The workers responded good naturedly agreeing that it might be a worthwhile idea to help clean up their language out of respect for the Sisters.

Coming into the circus culture requires time to establish trust. The tight-knit community takes time to fully embrace a newcomer. In that light, early in her circus ministry, Sister Dorothy had what she considered a stroke of genius. At the time she was often assigned to sell tickets during the afternoon prior to a performance. This job had a bit of down time when no one was there to purchase tickets. The ticket booth location was in a central location on the lot so other workers frequently had to pass the spot as they went about their tasks. Often individuals would stop for a few words with the new Sister. She sensed that some of them would have liked to say more but were hesitant. And then she bought a comfortable padded folding chair. She set her $15 investment down next to her booth and in no time she had visitors. Those with a heavy heart or a concern or just a need to talk with someone for awhile would pass her way, start to chat, and then sit down for a brief break and speak from their hearts. For Sister Dorothy, "Some people call it counseling. Some people call it mentoring. I call it being Church."[90]

---

90 Claudia McDonnell. "Three-Ring Vocation," *Catholic New York*, (April 2004) 40.

As soon as a level of trust is established between the Sisters and those with whom they work, the spiritual hungers of the circus people come pouring out. They request Bible Study, which like much of circus spiritual activity is often ecumenical or interfaith, individual spiritual guidance, prayer services, and assistance dealing with official church procedures. The latter often happens in connection with marriages. While the show was in Washington, D.C., a non-Catholic couple came to one of the Sisters saying that they wanted to get married because the immigration status of the young man had been finally resolved. He had some Baptist background. So, in the time between shows, Sister walked from the arena to the nearest Baptist Church. She persistently knocked on the pastor's door until an elderly minister answered. She proceeded to outline the situation and enlist the minister's support in helping the couple celebrate their union. He agreed, met with the couple and married them.

All the needs of the church community for Word, Worship, Service, and Community Building are the needs of the circus faith community. The circumstances call for ministers to orchestrate responses to these ordinary religious requirements with extraordinary creativity.

The Missionary Sisters of the Sacred Heart who work in the circus. Sister Dorothy Fabritze and Sister Bernard Overkamp, are women who have worked as missionaries in the jungles of Papua New Guinea, one for 16 years and the other for 25 years.[91] After coming to the awareness that the people of Papua New Guinea had developed their own Christian community well enough not to depend on foreign leadership, they moved on.

They left that mission field with no assurances of what would come next. In the process of seeking out a new missionary endeavor one of them came across a book for teaching religion in the circus setting. She casually dismissed the possibility of circus ministry but the idea surfaced again and she decided to explore it. It became clear that the circus was a migrant ministry with almost no ministers. These people were on the road from ten to twelve

---

91 Sister Dorothy, and I initially developed our longstanding friendship when we were both young members of the Missionary Sisters of the Sacred Heart. We shared community life prior to her years in Papua New Guinea and before my departure from the community.

months a year, frequently moving, constantly working, and almost completely on their own in meeting their religious needs.

Sister Dorothy decided on the circus life first, and then asked Sister Bernard if she felt God was calling her to come on the road as well. Sister Bernard said no, she didn't think so. She was open enough, however, to attend several circus performances and gradually, as she prayed about it and learned more about the needs of the people, the idea grew on her. She agreed to take on this challenge as well, originally for a one-year trial, but that was more than a decade ago. In her own words, "Here I am, and I have not regretted my decision."[92] As a missionary, Sister Bernard maintains, "We see that the needs of folks are changing. It's our job to find different places where they really need the word of God, or just acceptance and love."[93]

In the process of committing themselves to a radically new lifestyle, both Sisters have developed and expanded their own understanding of mission work. It is one thing to be geographically far from one's native land and enter into a relationship with a totally new culture. It is another to remain near to home and yet become part of a strikingly different culture. Both are dramatic calls to openness and responsiveness to others and radical trust in God.

Sister Dorothy said that she knew almost nothing about the circus when she entered into this field of ministry. As a child who went to the circus with her family she only paid attention to the all-important popcorn and cotton candy but had no idea of what really went into making the actual performance possible. Sister Bernard had just as little in the way of experience and so they both entered into a powerful learning experience when they began their circus careers.[94]

Many donors intrigued with this novel and potentially fruitful venture provided the funds for the Sisters to purchase a truck and a trailer. The small trailer consisted of two rooms in addition to a closet-sized bathroom. One room had a kitchenette, bunk beds, a

---

92 Claudia McDonnell. "Three-Ring Vocation," *Catholic New York*, (April 2004) 41.
93 Jennifer Warnick. "Two Traveling Nuns, Circus is a Calling," *The Herald*, (Seattle, Washington: October 2004).
94 Their exploration of possible mission work before choosing the circus included stints at Habitat for Humanity in Guatemala, a Native American reservation in New Mexico, an outreach center in West Virginia, and a half-way house for non-violent released prisoners in Pennsylvania.

table with benches, a couch and a chair. The second room was a bedroom. A talented friend transformed the bedroom into a chapel and they were ready to roll, living mostly in the other room and taking the bunk beds or the pull out couch as their resting places.

The transition was not easy but the Sisters soon found their niche and adapted to circus life. Early in their first year with the Roberts Brothers Circus, Sister Dorothy wrote in a letter, "It is the most tiring ministry I have LOVED in a long time. I was just telling Sr. Bernard every time I say "I love it" I wonder why. It is hard work to hitch and unhitch and move the 29-foot trailer every day. It is challenging to work 5 a.m. to 11 p.m. every day. It takes patience to wait for a day of one show to have a little free time. But truthfully I belong here. I came for the people and they have not disappointed me. They are kind and hospitable and we can help each other grow."[95]

Within their first two years, Sister Dorothy could articulate some of the reasons why the circus turned out to be such a good fit after living so long in Papua New Guinea. Referring to her return to the United States, she told a reporter, "It was traumatic to come back to this culture, my culture. By the time I got back, it was …a selfish – no, let's use the word consumer – culture….I needed a community culture, I think, and the circus is a community. People depend on each other for survival here, so I'm back where I belong."[96]

As of this writing the two Missionaries Sisters of the Sacred Heart are the only full-time ministers to provide religious formation, prayer experiences, and spiritual counseling in the United States' circus world. And despite the missionary aspect of their calling they do not seek to proselytize or convert anyone but rather support and encourage the faith of those they serve, no matter what that person's religious connections might be. Their motivation, in Sister Dorothy's words, is to "let people in this circus know that there's a God who cares about them no matter what's happened in their lives."[97] In that spirit they respond to requests from people of great faith who belong to various Christian denominations, Jewish, and

---

95   Sister Dorothy Fabritze. Letter written to Catherine and Robert Martin, (March 4, 2000).
96   Michael Leahy. *The Washington Post*, (May 4, 2000) 5E-6E.
97   Ibid.

Muslim believers, as well as to those who have no religious beliefs but who want to discuss the big questions of life.

A forty-three year old man who has often spoken to the Sisters and Father Jerry Hogan, the national circus chaplain, about spiritual realities believes primarily in the power of the individual and does not acknowledge a power outside of him. Yet he does not claim to be an atheist, which he considers a "terrible label." "What I like to explain to my friends who are clergy is that Christians, Muslims, Jews, you name it have faith that God exists. Atheists have faith that God does not exist. I have no such faith either way. I am not convinced that there is a God. That does not make me an agnostic. It's a grey area with which unfortunately language has limitations…. I'm trying to find words for something that's very difficult to explain in this language that we use."[98]

A fifty-one year old man who has become disenchanted with religion, goes to one of the Sisters for spiritual conversations and Bible study. After proclaiming, "What people do in the name of religion is disgusting," he continued, "Then I met Sister Dorothy and she is just a remarkable woman, and Sister Bernard. The two of them truly practice what they preach….And they have kind of restored my faith if you will….There is a power greater than us. I don't know what it is and I don't really care about what it is if it drives people like Sister Dorothy to be who they are, I'm all for it." Teresa Earl, a circus owner who worked with the Sisters early in their traveling career considered, "Any circus has hard times. It takes faith to keep doing this. I'm not Catholic, but it's an ecumenical message that the sisters are sending."[99]

There are innumerable individual spiritual counseling opportunities and the chance to reach out to those looking for some simple assistance. A thirty-eight year old woman smiled as she told me, "Sister gives me little booklets that have something for every day to read before you go to sleep." One man who was going through a relational break up told me, "I'm a bit heartbroken at the moment but I will survive through the help of God, if you will with

---
98 Because of his upbringing, this man sees himself as more independent than others. He finds it difficult to share his views with them, because although, "We are taught that honesty is the best policy. People don't want honesty. They want a beautiful lie."
99 Michael Leahy. *The Washington Post*, (May 4, 2000) 5E-6E.

the help of Sister Dorothy. I may not everyday get on my knees and pray to God but I feel like I'm communicating to Him through this wonderful woman. She is … a voice of the real God, not the vengeful one which I never believed in.… God is love, that's what's always made sense to me, and Sister Dorothy loves, period. And just being in her presence you feel loved. You feel calmed. You feel cared for, which is what the church community, in its ideal form is supposed to do…"

The approximately thirty-five young women dancers in Ringling Brothers Circus turn to Sister Bernard as they would to a grandmother. She comforts them in their homesickness and encourages them in their desire to make good and loving choices. She repairs their shoes and sews up the tears in their costumes; laughs in the presence of their exuberance and shores them up in their troubles. Sister Bernard says, "My ministry is to be with the young girls, listen to them, listen to their stories, listen to their heartaches."[100]

A middle-aged man expressed his opinion that his experience of the spirituality of the Sisters restored his lost faith and gave him this insight. "I think they need more women, to be honest with you, in higher levels in religion. This is the day and age we need that. The men have screwed it up. Not saying the women wouldn't do it either but gosh, give it a chance."

A mother of two children knew that Sister worked with the youngsters but was not sure if she would set up regular time with an adult. She got up the courage to ask and they met once a week over a two-year period. She recalled the beginning. "I had been really searching for God. I was brought up Catholic and went to Church every week but I think as I formed my own family and as I got older, you know, the interest in God grew stronger.… I had a lot of questions.… So, I've had a lot of my questions answered. You know, or not even answered, but just a way to … deal with things, life on the road. I've really learned to talk to God throughout the day… so I can definitely say God's a big part of my life right now. She has been a tremendous help in that."

---

100 Martina Hart. "Circus Sisters," *Living City*, (October 2009, Vol. 48 No. 10) 16.

The Sisters have also arranged for many formal services as well as individual counseling sessions when requested to do so. They have conducted the Rite of Christian Initiation of Adults, assisted parents seeking the Baptism of their children, and have prepared adults and young people for Baptism, Eucharist, Confirmation, and Reconciliation. Once when Sister Dorothy was conducting a First Eucharist preparation session for children, an adult passing by poked her head in and said, "I need Eucharist, too." Another session was soon added to the weekly schedule to accommodate the new candidate.

Regular religious education is presented for the children on a weekly basis. The advantage is that they are usually small groups, so there is a lot of individualized attention. The challenge is that all the youngsters are taught by the same person. Parents are expected to play the key role in their child's faith formation even when their youngster goes to formal catechetical sessions. A thirty-four year old mother wrote about her daughter: "Everything she learns with Sr. Dorothy she tells me. We talk about it. She comes home and sings songs about Jesus. She has it in her heart now. We pray together. I pray in Spanish then she prays in English. I teach her to believe in God, believe in herself…. She has religious books and movies to watch." Another woman of a similar age also remarked on her daughter's new habit of singing to or talking about Jesus spontaneously during the day. She described her response. "I'm wowed by it because I know I didn't do that or I don't remember at that age doing it. But I think she already has a really good understanding of Jesus."

One couple who come from different Christian denominations want their daughter to choose her own religion when she is older but, the mother said, right now "She is going to Sr. Dorothy. I want her to learn, pray, believe there is a God."

There is generally a religious education class or a sacramental preparation class held every day after work, five days a week. When the adult or children candidates are ready for a sacramental celebration, the Sisters work to find a local priest who is willing to preside in the town the circus will be performing in just when those preparations are completed.

Those who benefit from the Sisters' sacramental ministry see it as a special blessing. Many have yearned for years to celebrate Eucharist, Confirmation, or Matrimony but have never had access to an itinerant catechist to travel with them on their journey physically as well as spiritually. Having an experienced person of faith minister to their need for richer ritual expression of their connection to the church community is a well-appreciated grace. One couple whom one of the Sisters prepared for a long-awaited celebration of matrimony marked the one-year anniversary of their wedding by sending a Paschal candle to the Sisters as an expression of their gratitude. They had come to know that Baptismal source of their sacramental union as husband and wife in Christ. The Easter candle, symbol of their life together in Christian marriage, became a fitting way to say thank you to the spiritual guide who led them to that wisdom.

When one woman was ready for her First Reconciliation, she was a bit nervous, but Sister had found a priest who spoke the woman's native Spanish, and the Sisters offered to have the celebration in their trailer. The woman's husband and a few friends came along. Everyone chatted in the kitchen/sitting area while the woman sat with the priest in the Sisters' chapel, which was now a Reconciliation Room. Afterwards, the whole group celebrated with some coffee cake freshly baked by one of the Sisters for the occasion.

Whenever possible, the Sisters research and let people know where and when Mass will be available near where the circus will be quartered in each town. Coordinating worship opportunities on the circus premises requires considerable planning. The Sisters contact priests in towns to which they will be traveling to see if they can find someone willing to come to the circus to offer Mass under the unusual circumstances that entails, i.e., one-half hour maximum, at a specified time available in between shows, in a makeshift room or at the bottom of a staircase. Sometimes the Mass in English, sometimes in Spanish, but both languages are usually incorporated into the celebration in some way.

Community religious experiences require real space for the bodies who will participate. Finding physical space for any religious activity in the circus work is often a challenge. But some ministerial services can be offered without a select site. On one show, a worker asked Sister to give him a Bible verse to carry with him each day. She wrote it out at night and gave it to him. Not long after another person heard about this and then another and, in a short time, she was writing out ten copies of a Bible verse on individual slips of paper each evening before she went to bed. The next day she would distribute them as the petitioners came to pick up their Scriptural inspiration.

One of the most public religious acts the Sisters were asked to do was in their very first circus. The owner surprised Sister Dorothy by saying she wanted to start each performance with prayer. So, at every show, the curtain would open, the audience applauded as the Ringmaster appeared. Then he would announce Sister Dorothy who would come running into the center ring with a microphone in her hand. Before the bowed heads in the audience, she prayed aloud and from her heart with thanks and praise and asked God's blessing on all present, with a special petition for the safety of the performers. Applause followed. Then the show would begin. A newscast which captured one of those moments also shows footage of people thanking Sister after the show for praying before the show.

The same owner, Teresa Earl, who assigned prayer duty in the ring, became especially fond of Sister Dorothy and Sister Bernard. Later she asked them to be her sponsors when she decided to become a member of the Catholic Church. The possibility of joining the Catholic community had been in her mind for many years. She finally acted on her desire because she saw that Catholics demonstrated an interest in circus life.

Much as in non-circus parish life, not all of the service provided is specifically oriented to religion. One of the requests Sister Dorothy has responded to in every circus in which she has worked, is to teach English to those for whom it is not their home language. In some circuses, parents have enlisted Sister to tutor their children in school subjects with which they were having difficulty. Some say the Sisters provide a kind of practical advice service: "They can network; tell you who to go to."

A young woman mentioned that the presence of the Sisters provided some comfort for those she had left behind in her native country. Her priest who knew her from the time of her Baptism was particularly worried. "Now he is happy. I told him there are God-people there."

The Missionary Sisters of the Sacred Heart were preceded in circus ministry by The Little Sisters of Jesus. In fact, during her discernment period, Sister Dorothy lived, traveled, and worked with Little Sisters Jo and Priscilla. Their three weeks together on the circus confirmed Sister Dorothy's decision that this was her call also.

Members of the community of the Little Sisters have a charism or special spirit of dedication to nomadic peoples. They follow the vision of their foundress, Little Sister Magdeleine who had a heart for vagabonds and the like-minded, Charles de Foucauld, who influenced her dedication to those whose lifestyle is one of constant movement from place to place.

One of the Little Sisters who has served the circus community in the United States said, "I feel God present throughout the day, 'Nomad' with me. I agree with our foundress who said she felt closest to God on the road." The ministry of presence is part of their special charism. They share life with people without attempting to proselytize.

A circus friend of the Little Sisters remarked on her first meal with the Little Sisters. "The Sisters invited us to dinner. My husband said, 'Hon, we are going to get lectured.' But that was not the case at all. I mean not even a little." The vocation of the Little Sisters is to live among and be one with those whom they serve in prayer, companionship, and compassion.

One of the Little Sisters, Sister Priscilla, was actually born in a circus in Switzerland. However, her father died in an accident when she was four and the remaining family left the circus to live with other relatives.

A circus minister for thirty years, one of the Little Sisters recalled her entry into this apostolate: "When the idea came up to start a group of us traveling here in the States, I offered to look for some information, sent it to our General Council, was asked to help get it started...and never left. The fact that I felt 'right at home' with the people and the rhythm of life from the start has little by little helped me to discover my own nomadic roots and cherish them as a precious gift. At the time of my final vows (1982) I made a special mention in my consecration of giving my life for my brothers and sisters in the circus, side shows, and carnivals."

These dedicated women religious identify with the people among whom they live. The power of this for those whom they serve is evident to all and is highly valued by the circus people. With the same spirit of hospitality and love as the Missionary Sisters of the Sacred Heart exhibit, the Little Sisters are entirely open to those of any or no religious affiliation.

On their visit to an emergency room, the unchurched circus-working parents of a sick child were asked their religion. They only answered, "We have the nuns." The Little Sisters of Jesus were part of the circus and were experienced as the religious anchor of their community.

One of the Little Sisters said, "We have the chapel and try to let folks know it's there and open and they are welcome. We try to keep our trailer uncluttered and with a certain simplicity about it, bright and welcoming, a place to come and warm up, have a coffee, find a sympathetic ear or a bandaid."

Maurice Zundel, priest, theologian, and liturgist called the circus the "liturgy of the people." He came up with this phrase after visiting with some Little Sisters at a circus in Lausanne, Switzerland. He was particularly impressed with the ministry of these women religious. He saw them as "enlightening the whole life of the circus artists, without a word, by the presence of God which breathes in them."[101]

The three Little Sisters of Jesus who welcomed the MSC Sisters into circus ministry no longer live and work there on a full time basis.[102] However, two of the Sisters, Little Sister Jo and Little Sister Priscilla continue to minister to circus people for significant

---

101 Maurice Zundel. *Wonder and Poverty*, (Sherbrooke, QC: *Éditions Paulines*, 1993). This book is the text of a retreat preached by Maurice Zundel in 1963.
102 All of the Little Sisters and Missionary Sisters of the Sacred Heart who work in the circus are more than 63 years old.

stretches of time throughout the year. They downsized by selling their trailer to a circus family with whom they are friends and obtained an even smaller vehicle. Now they work part time, doing spot dates, which means going out to work in various circuses for a month or two at a time. One of those who previously shared circus life with them said, "I know Sister Jo. She doesn't say it but she misses being on the road.... And I know Sister Priscilla doesn't want to quit."

They share the challenge of ministry faced by those who are deeply attached to the people with whom they serve while aware that their efforts are becoming more difficult to sustain. But even when they cannot share the physical journey of the circus community as often as they would like, the Little Sisters find ways to continue to share their spiritual journey.

In addition to intermittent stays in various circuses throughout the traveling season, the Little Sisters keep in communication with their many circus friends by writing, emailing, and calling on a regular basis. The letters are filled with news not only of the sisters but of their friends in various circus communities. Their deep spirituality comes through in the way they write and the words they use. Little Sister Jo will occasionally include one of her image-rich poems which capture her experience of God at work in the muddy lots as well as the center ring of the circus world. There are many testimonials to the effectiveness of the ministry of these Sisters in their over 25 years of service with the circus.

One woman described them as "the Little Sisters who lived and worked to help the workers know God cares."

A sixty-five year old man simply said, "We have been lucky in the past to have Little Sisters with the shows we have been with." Another man called them "a God gift."

A fifty-eight year old woman said one of the things that helped her maintain a spiritual life in the circus was "being with the Little Sisters on the Kelly-Miller Circus; sharing our spiritual thoughts, concerns."

A priest who spent some time with the circus remembered, "When the Little Sisters were on the show we would gather with some of the show folks and discuss the Sunday readings."

The Sisters also brought prayer to bear at times of crisis within the circus community. One woman remembered, "There were three brothers on Carson and Barnes, and one of the guys got sick. He went home to Mexico and they had services, I think it was every night for two weeks for him."

Referring to another event, a woman told me, "They had services a lot....When a fellow died; I went into that service....Most everybody on the show went."

The Scriptures provided a focus for regular gatherings with the Sisters for the nine years they were on the Carson and Barnes circus. One of the Sisters wrote, "We often got together with a little group for weekly Gospel Sharing or "Lectio Divina" with 3-5 others. Sometimes the schedule is difficult to work around to do so unless we have it rather late at night, 10:30-12:00 pm."

An older woman recalled other spiritual opportunities. "When the Little Sisters were on the show, they would on occasion have a local priest come and say Mass. Also our group on Fridays for Communion service." When asked if he ever talks to God or prays, one man said, "Yes, especially after the Little Sisters joined Carson and Barnes." Then he referred to the Friday gatherings as well where, he reported, "A group of us met ...to pray, sing, and receive the host."

For a while, when they were still part of the Carson and Barnes circus, they were fortunate to have as music minister a circus member who gathered a "little choir, complete with guitars, bass guitar, drums, trumpets, and soloists" for the services.

Much of their influence, however, was outside of formal religious services. They built close relationships with other circus folks wherever they lived. One woman who admitted thinking of God "when I'm driving, of course and sometimes when I'm walking to the cookhouse," still considered herself "not a very religious person, as some people are. I'm a low scale." Yet she considered Little Sisters Jo and Priscilla very close to her family and herself: "They spent time in our house.... We parked next to them. We shared food back and forth a lot. We've really been good friends." An older man said, "The Little Sisters of Jesus give us help and hope."

A thirty-year old woman recalled the hospitality the community of Little Sisters extended to her during a time of need. "When I was a teenager, my mom had a bad accident in Reno, Nevada. She fell from the trapeze and broke both her hands. They took me to a convent with the Little Sisters. I went with them to houses to try to help people."

Ministry is always a two-way relationship with profound effects on the designated minister as well as the one being served. Many have remarked that the one serving often receives more than he or she gives. From their perspective, the Little Sisters see themselves as evangelized in certain significant ways by their association with the circus community.

One of the Little Sisters wrote to others in her religious community of some ways in which circus life coincides with the charism they all share with one of their primary spiritual guides, Brother Charles de Foucauld. Little Sister Jo highlighted the movement from town to town as a "good school in both detachment and living the present moment." Frequently experiencing the simplicity of children coming to the circus, she said, "reminds us of the child asleep in each of us and the necessity to become like little children to enter the Kingdom of Heaven." Reflecting on unity, she wrote, "Among circus folks (a small but very diverse group of people as far as nationality, race, age, temperament, religion, etc. go) there is a deep sense of mutual acceptance and tolerance toward each other and for the common project. We have much to learn from this." And on laughter and joy, she concluded, "The clown helps us in a non-threatening way to laugh at ourselves and to see humor in our weaknesses and blunders, discovering in them a source of humility and joy. Here, too, is a reminder for us to look at life with Gospel eyes in which the world's values are a bit topsy-turvy."[103]

---

[103] Letter sent by Little Sister Jo to her religious community from Arborg, Manitoba, Canada, while on the road with the Kelly Miller Circus, (July 22, 1992).

In addition to the circus nuns there are other ministers as well. While not actually living the circus life, Father George "Jerry" Hogan has been the national chaplain to those on the circus since 1993.[104] An ambitious pastor of a very large and active parish in the Boston Archdiocese, Fr. Jerry always has the circus people in his heart. He is a type of bridge between two groups who are each sometimes considered on the fringe of normal life. In his own words, "People think circus people are strange and others think religious people are strange, so we're really breaking down barriers."[105]

He travels up to 60,000 miles a year to visit the various circuses across the country whenever he can. He takes the time to listen, to talk, to celebrate sacraments, to lead memorial services for those who have died, to bless, to preach, and to encourage. A sixty-four year old woman said, "When there is a problem and Father Jerry or one of the other circus religious leaders is there they have a significant impact on circus spiritual life for Catholics and non-Catholics alike." Father Jerry calls the service of those working with traveling entertainers the ministry of the moment. It means being there in the midst of people and responding as opportunities arise. In his own words, "The ministry of the moment can have many different twists and turns, from hearing a Confession behind a Lion's cage, blessing a carousel, to leading 50,000 people in prayer at the start of a Grand Prix Auto Race."[106] Speaking of both Father Jerry and the Sisters, one man remarked that he goes to some of the services offered mainly because, "They're good people and they're ministering to people who desperately need it."

The harmony of the ministry of the circus Sisters and Fr. Jerry is highlighted in the times when one of the circuses with the Sisters is scheduled to be near Fr. Jerry's Parish.

On one such occasion the plan was to have the young people preparing for First Eucharist and Confirmation celebrate their

---

104 Father Hogan is the fourth national circus chaplain ever appointed by the United States Conference of Catholic Bishops. The request for such a minister came from members of the Ringling Brothers and Barnum and Bailey Circus after Father Ed Sullivan died. Father Sullivan was a highly respected priest who started the tradition of traveling as a spiritual guide and friend in the United States circus community. "The Church's Circus Tradition," *St. Anthony Messenger*, (May 2002) 17.
105 Kristen Moulton. "Big top ministry," *The Salt Lake Tribune*, (October 2, 2004) C2.
106 George "Jerry" Hogan. "Hospitality of the Church in the United States Towards the Circus and Traveling Show People," *People on the Move*, (December 2005, No. 99 Supplement).

great moment at the parish church instead of in an empty room backstage at the local arena. With their families present and Father Jerry presiding, the young people would also express their joy in a liturgical dance which Sister had taught them to perform as a processional. Everything seemed perfect.

Then two surprises worthy of being attributed to the Holy Spirit occurred. The parents of two children preparing for their sacraments, one First Eucharist and one Confirmation, told Sister Dorothy that they wanted to have their fourteen-year civil marriage celebrated as a Sacrament in the Church. Sr. Dorothy agreed and then was humbled by their request that she do some marriage preparation with them. Their marriage was obviously working and she would have little to say on that subject but she agreed to meet with them and discuss the spirituality of married life. They were both very happy to find a time to meet each week. Sister Dorothy also began to plan how she would incorporate the celebration of their marriage into the liturgy for the great day of celebration.

That same week, an English-speaking Brazilian dancer came to Sister Dorothy and said that there were four other Portuguese women who would like to prepare for Confirmation. When the language issue was raised, the young woman said that she had been a catechist for young people in Brazil and she would be glad to do the preparation if Sister would guide her in the process. With inspiring fervor the young woman made sure that the candidates got their Baptismal certificates from Brazil and she obtained Portuguese language catechetical materials. She and Sister met to go over the lessons and the catechist and her candidates met every Friday before the show. The young woman herself thanked Sister Dorothy for the opportunity because she said it helped her grow in her own closeness to Jesus.

The enthusiasm for the Liturgy being planned spread beyond the circle of candidates and catechists. Catholic and non-Catholic circus friends and acquaintances made arrangements to be at the celebration. Members of the circus band offered their talents. The keyboardist agreed to play the church organ, if Sister would set the stop tabs. The trumpeter also added his special sounds to the festivities. After all this, the final Fall celebration with Father Jerry became the joyous culmination of a grace-filled community formation experience.

Besides the regular pastoral ministry of Father Jerry, numerous other ministers support the Sisters in their work. Chief among these are a network of understanding priests across the country who generously agree to celebrate Eucharist on site for the migrant circus folks.[107] Others include a few religious congregations who share their convent homes with the circus Sisters along the road. This provides several evenings a year as a respite from trailer life and a chance to share occasional brief snippets of life with other members of religious communities.

The ministry of religious formation in the Catholic community was being done by at least one woman on the circus before the Sisters arrival in their present troupe. She was delighted to have the women religious join the circus community. Now this catechist has moved onto another circus where she continues to combine her circus work with a ministry of preparing young people for the celebration of the sacraments.

The Missionaries of the Sacred Heart dedicate much of their time at present traveling from circus to circus to develop catechists who will continue the work of formation after the sisters are no longer able to do this ministry. This new direction of their circus ministry is called SPEC, Show People's Evangelization of Catechists. One of these potential catechists experienced the power of ministry when she met a friend from another circus. She could not get over how different he seemed. The transformation she saw as an inner peace was a mystery until he explained that he had just finished a year of preparation by being confirmed. He expressed a conviction that the formation and sacramental celebration had changed him dramatically.

The staff of the United States Conference of Catholic Bishops (USCCB) former Office of Pastoral Care of Migrants and Refugees (now under the umbrella of the USCCB Secretariat of Cultural Diversity in the Church) worked with Father Jerry Hogan to create a catechetical book for circus use. It is titled "On the Road with Jesus." They also prepared and distributed a circus prayer book,

---

107 The cadre of those who have presided at mass on-site for the circus includes a Bishop, two cloistered monks, members of other religious communities, and diocesan priests. There have, however, been occasional refusals from local clerics who consider the circus environment an improper setting for the celebration of Eucharist.

"Journeying with the Lord," aimed specifically at the particular concerns in a traveling show milieu. With the support of the USCCB, the National Circus Chaplain Office of Circus Ministry also publishes a newsletter, "The Troubadour," which serves the circus, traveling show and race car communities.[108]

Those who minister to the people in migrating entertainment, including the carnival and rodeo circuits have banded together as "The Circus and Traveling Show Ministries." Father Jerry Hogan is a key figure in this group. Their mission statement proclaims,

> We are a national body of Christian men and women (clergy, religious and lay) who serve as pastoral ministers among all persons called to work in the American traveling entertainment industries. We provide a ministry of presence by affirming the love of God among them, sharing in their lives, and offering direct services, worship and advocacy. We carry out this ministry through full and part-time employment in the industries and by volunteer services. This work is supported by the United States Conference of Catholic Bishops, as part of its pastoral concern for people on the move. We network, communicate and gather annually to support one another in our involvement with the traveling entertainment industries. Our goals include: Improvement of catechetical and pastoral services through empowerment of those we serve. Support for efforts to improve quality of life in these areas: Educational/Literacy; Housing; Retirement and Elder Care; Health Care; Immigration; Work Satisfaction and an Affirming Environment; Development and utilization of resources to enhance the ministry.

The retirement project referred to is a high priority of the group but one which requires more resources than they have been able to muster to date. The plan is to find and purchase land and

---

108 Some staff members have a history of providing additional support for the ministers when they can. While I was on an overnight with the circus in Washington, DC, Sister Charlotte Hobelman, SND, former staff member of what was then called "The Office of Pastoral Care for Migrants and Refugees," came to visit Sisters Dorothy and Bernard in their trailer. She came with a massive box of religious education materials and supplies from glitter to construction paper to scissors and so on, which she had gathered as donations. Sister Charlotte also arranged to take the circus Sisters for a drive through the Virginia countryside to enjoy a picnic lunch on a day when there was only one performance scheduled.

set up affordable housing where elderly and infirm members of the Circus community can live. The fulfilled dream would be, according to one member of the ministry group, a place "where circus folks no longer on the road can park together." Residents could continue to live together as part of the community of which they have been a part for so long. She added that the hope was "that this might also be a place where we could gather some circus folks for a kind of retreat or faith sharing – but we are not 'there' yet." Eventually the hope is to have a type of retirement village with some small buildings for assisted living. Support for this project has come from at least one performer. Dorothy Herbert is donating the proceeds from her memoir to the Circus and Traveling Shows Retirement Project, Inc.[109]

As indicated earlier, at present the only full-time circus ministers are Sister Dorothy Fabritze and Sister Bernard Overcamp. They too are close to retirement. All of the circus Sisters, both the Little Sisters of Jesus and the Missionaries of the Sacred Heart, Father Jerry, and members of the staff of the USCCB's Secretariat of Cultural Diversity in the Church make an effort to bring the message of the need for additional circus ministers to members of religious congregations and their associate members as well as to Bishops and priests across the United States. They are eager to let people know what circus life is like and to wake generous disciples to the great need for ministers to this community. "The harvest is abundant but the laborers are few." (Luke 10:2)

Circus ministry is an entertainment ministry, providing pastoral care to those who move others to become aware of the beauty, strength, and happiness that are possible within the human community. One of the current ministers says that the initial orientation for any new potential circus ministers should be to go and see a show first. It would say to the one considering such a vocation, "This is the joy your work can help to provide for those who are too busy, too stressed, too tired, or too sad to celebrate the great gift of just being alive."

---

[109] Concern for elderly and infirm circus folks is evident in the work of Dorita Ricker, a member of the Circus and Traveling Shows Ministry organization. She has already compiled and distributed a practical directory of Senior Services available for retired circus personnel.

When a circus does not have people acting consciously in a ministerial role, spirituality and prayer do not cease. However, they become, for many, less focused, somewhat more impoverished, and less connected to the larger community of faith. A forty-five year old man gave this appraisal, "We have little free time and no spiritual guidance, though when someone visits us once in awhile it helps us a lot." Another said, "I really think that all of us are missing a permanent spiritual guide. It would be good to have regular visits of some sort, not just ones that are sporadic. It reminds me of God in everything that happens around us."

The community can remain scattered without a focal leader. Pastoral ministers tend to draw out those seeking a more vivid connection with God. A thirty-one year old woman who formerly skated in an ice show concluded, "I think here on the circus it is a huge blessing that we have Sister Dorothy and Sister Bernard. I think they keep a lot of people grounded. ...You can see it in people. They just don't have guidance, there's just a lot of outside influence....So having a spiritual person here, for me, has eliminated a lot of the negative side of being on the road."

As a parent now, this woman also values the faith formation available to her children when the Sisters are on hand. The faithful seek assistance in sharing their faith tradition with their children. Circus parents want the best for their children, they want spiritual assistance, but they need flexibility in making that happen.

They also express their desire to celebrate those actions which will mark them as officially in coherence with the larger faith community. People of faith identify the spiritual needs they wish to fulfill without programmatic direction from a minister but they require trust in this faith representative to request any assistance which would help them fulfill their spiritual needs. Spiritual and earthly realities of life are not divorced in experience. Therefore, those who trust the religious leader will present their personal, family, and job concerns along with their religious needs to a caring minister.

A non-Catholic accountant on the circus gave her assessment of the effect of having a professional religious leader on site. "If you need something or know someone who does and

Father Jerry or Father David or someone else is there, you go to them because they are there and they don't want anything. They just want to help."[110]

Being there and being there to serve are the core aspects of circus ministry as seen in the lives of the current people who have responded to this call. Increasingly the circus ministers will come from within the circus milieu. Those who have entered into this life from outside the community have become circus people themselves. Now as they move forward in their own spiritual journey, they have begun to form the people from within who can take on the leadership of faith formation and sacred celebration. In the tradition of the Little Sisters of Jesus, the Missionary Sisters of the Sacred Heart, Father Jerry Hogan, and all those others who minister in the circus, those who continue this work will need to develop the ministry of presence and the ministry of the moment.

Those two models of ministry are found beyond the circus world of course. But their existence in circus life is a reminder of the grace they bestow on the minister as well as the community. Looking at another aspect of circus ministry may have significant implications for other ministries as well. The nature of circus ministry as it is currently lived by those who serve in this capacity is ministry to a total community, regardless of religious affiliation. It has an ecumenical, inter-faith, all-embracing aspect to its service which could be an effective model for others who seek to minister in faith and love. It is being there and being there to serve anyone within the circle of the community. Spiritual and corporal works of mercy intertwine. One counsels while clothing the unclothed in a costume wardrobe room. Another instructs while feeding the hungry at a concession stand. At one time one visits the imprisoned or the sick; at another one buries the dead and comforts the afflicted. In the circus realm, only certain folks enter into specific religious actions but the minister is there for the whole community of persons and for the wholeness of the body-spirit persons who share the circus life together.

---

110 Father David Tetrault is an Episcopalian priest who has spent time working in the circus and ministering to circus folks. He continues his commitment to the circus and is a member of the "Circus and Traveling Show Ministries" group.

Servant-Leader God touches us through others; calls forward those who wash each other's feet, anoints them for compassionate care. Back-stage God provides the grace for ministers to multiply the bread and fish each traveler brings to the gathering; to nourish those who in turn can take God's love to larger circles beneath the cosmic canopy.

CHAPTER 7

Performance is Meant to be a Gift of Love

> *"Their voice goes out through all the earth, and their message to the ends of the world. High above he pitched a tent for the sun, who comes out of his pavilion like a bridegroom, exulting like a hero to run his race."* (Psalm 19:4-5)

High overhead the trapeze artists wave to the crowd. The broad-shouldered catcher is languidly swinging back and forth. He drops downward, gripping the swing with his legs while his arms reach out. A lithe figure takes to the other swing. They rise and fall until the rhythm is just right. A signal is sounded and the woman jumps out into the air, suspended, then the arms grasp her and she is safely brought home to the aerial platform. The audience is rapt. We are that daring artist. We have felt the call to take a chance in our lives, to leap into some dangerous expanse, and, at this moment, we know that it just might work. Facing our fears, taking a risk, suddenly seems worth trying. We are thrilled by the daring. We are awed by the courage and skill and strength. Life is hard. Life is great.

The jugglers stride onto the floor. One by one the young couple tosses objects back and forth to one another. The first few catches of several items receive appreciative applause. But, then there are more, and more added, and the jugglers spin as they catch some, take some behind their backs, and others under their legs.

The appreciation becomes amazement. How much more can they handle? Ah, how much more can any of us handle in the balancing act of life? They do their act with grace and a smile. When they bobble a catch, they graciously pick up and go on with the show. We applaud. We are reminded of the truth. Life is busy. Life can be a lot of fun.

The clown ambles forward in oversized shoes. Life has its difficulties and suffering. We cannot always figure things out but, in the end, our problems are often not as big as we think they are. We can laugh at ourselves. We can be happy.

Circus people are not itinerant loners looking to relieve the local populace of their money before packing up and leaving town in the middle of the night. They are people of the performing arts. They are a unique group within the entertainment field. They are modern day troubadours who liven up the crossroads of the successive towns through which they pass.

The center ring is a sacred space. It is a place of mystery and ritual. It is performative space set aside for the presentation of a thrilling spectacle. It is meant not only to be seen by but to involve with awe and laughter all those whose seats create a larger circle embracing the artists within.

Robert Lax speaks for the circus ensemble, when he writes, "By day from town to town we carry Eden in our tents and bring its wonders to the children who have lost their dream of home."[111]

The performance is one of the significant elements of circus life that enhances the spiritual experience of those who prepare and present the show. One clown talked about the paradox between the pressures against living a spiritual life flowing from the demands of the performance and the energy leading to a deeper spiritual life that results from bringing the performance to completion. "When I get into the spirituality of it …we are actively participating in the creation of joy and joy brings glory to God according to the Bible, doesn't it? …Just by what we're doing, we're participating in something which is spiritual…. There is a great sacrifice in circus … but it's all from love."

---

[111] Robert Lax. *Circus Days and Nights*, (Woodstock, NY: The Overlook Press, 2000) 51.

Part of the sacrifice is to prepare a body which can express the full potential of its beauty and power. The training, practice, stretching, exercise, and experimentation which result in a grace-filled demonstration before the audience require phenomenal dedication. The great ease of the flowing motions of acrobats, trapeze artists, dancers, and high wire performers comes at a great cost. It is a cost, however, paid freely and generously.

Some critique the danger inherent in many circus acts. Those observers fear that performers unnecessarily threaten their safety for an insufficient reason. e.e. cummings, on the other hand, identified circus boldness and daring as an expression of living life to its fullest, with courage and strength. In *I: Six Nonlectures*, he said:

> damn everything but the circus! ... damn everything that is grim, dull, motionless, unrisking, inward turning, damn everything that won't get into the circle, that won't enjoy, that won't throw its heart into the tension, surprise, fear and delight of the circus, the round world, the full existence...[112]

A missionary priest visiting the circus reflected that the circus performance participates in the redemptive work of Christ in releasing people from their sadness and burdens, freeing them to the joy of life.

Circus people are part of a great common project to create something of beauty for many people. Every aspect of the performance is choreographed and executed with an eye to eliciting delight. Sam Keen's comments on one type of act are representative of all authentic circus presentations. "Trapeze is *not* primarily about defying death, courting danger, or taking risks. It is about creating beauty.... If the movement isn't graceful, it isn't right. Beauty is not optional."[113]

Every element of the composite is meant to complement the rest. The musicians select their pieces to enhance the mood of each varied act. The flowing movements of those on the chiffons are accompanied by sweet stringed sounds. A sustained drum roll

---
112 Edward Estlin Cummings. *I: Six Nonlectures*, (Harvard: Harvard University Press, 1953), p. 79.
113 Sam Keen. *Learning to Fly: Trapeze – Reflections on Fear, Trust, and the Joy of Letting Go*, (New York: Broadway Books, 1999) 75.

heightens the tension before an audacious performer is shot from a cannon. Enthusiastic horns and percussions bring the crowd to its feet for the grand finale.[114]

It is a work whose completion transcends the unique contributions of each person involved in its production. With all the implications for their lives and relationships, the quality of the circus show is extremely important to everyone involved in its production. From youngest to oldest, one of the first questions they will ask when you are first introduced, is "Have you seen the show yet?"

For some circus performance is a more than a career, it is a vocation, a calling to reveal God who is beauty and power, creative force and grandeur. They have come to the circus for a myriad of reasons, to be the sixth, seventh, or eighth generation of their family to live circus life, to follow a loved one, because they met a circus person who influenced them to try the life, because they were out of work and looking for a job, or to have a new experience, adventure, and travel to see new places.

The lure of being a part of the grand circus performance has drawn some to leave high-level salaries behind and others to join the company after successfully completing their college degrees. A musician told me, "I considered this a detour but I've been here for fifteen years now." One fifty-one year old man admitted, "I loved being in front of a crowd....I loved the friendships made within the circus and the people we came in contact with on the road."

There might frequently be a combination of motivations. As one young woman said, "I joined to kind of get away from the same thing every day. I grew up taking care of my family. This was for me. It was supposed to be for a couple of months. I fell in love. Now I'm here for different reasons." Another said she came, "as a life experience, because I love to dance, to make money, and to practice English." One man says the schedule is one of the most appealing things about the circus for him. Everything is structured and he does not have to put energy into that aspect of life.

A forty-seven year old life-long circus member explained, "I always said, if my parents would have been carpenters, I might be

---

[114] And in an emergency, the band's rendition of *Alexander's Ragtime Band*, gives everyone the signal that a critical situation is at hand.

making beautiful furniture now. Instead, I grew up in the circus and learned to be an aerialist." Without sophisticated spiritual analysis, another woman said she sees her work as, "my vocation, as well as a way of life." Another simply said she "felt called."

A twenty-five year old woman looking for a job came to the circus quite accidentally but in a way that she experienced as a call from God. "I was messing around on the Internet because I was bored. I didn't want the circus because of the image of scary people. I applied for Wardrobe at Disney on Ice,[115] but I prayed and said, "God, if you want me to go, have them offer me a job and next day they did."

The history of the circus dates back to the late Eighteenth Century. From that time until now, no matter what the reason for their arrival, life for all of those who join the circus has revolved around the presentation of an imaginative and awe-inspiring performance. An older man was clear about why he joined the circus because of his "desire to be a part of this unique art form and way of life. Circus represents many values which I consider important." A married couple who have spent many years as professional clowns said, "We joined the circus to travel and to entertain children, to bring laughter to others." Another woman simply said, "I love to perform aerial work."

One clown, whose form of entertainment predates the more recent history of the circus, expressed the spiritual gift offered by his profession in a particularly poetic way. "Children are amazed at everything. They live in a spherical world. As we get older, we become socialized. Life becomes a narrow corridor not a splendid palace. We are living for the next moment. Our life is horizontal. We hit a wall. ...Clowns, I believe, live in a vertical space. They live in *this* moment. In the time and space you spend with a clown, you are not going forward. At that moment you can apply to divinity."

The role of the audience is integral to the circus reality. It is not just important to have a big crowd in order to cover payroll costs. The enthusiasm of those viewing the show is extremely important. The whole project rests on a relationship in which the efforts of

---

115 Owned by Feld Entertainment, Inc., the same company that produces the Ringling Brothers and Barnum and Bailey Circus.

those presenting a performance interact with those who attend. Without an audience there is no dialogue. The troupe attempts to bring joy and release from mundane worries to children and adults alike. In fact, the desire to delight and take those present into the freedom of the world of imagination, is clear from the moment the Ringmaster intones the opening invitation of the show to "boys and girls, children of all ages."

In their turn, audience members affirm the value of the circus community's existence and efforts. Laughter, smiles, sounds of relief and amazement, embraces within families, all encourage and uplift performers, owners, and the support staff as well. Signs of approval uplift the company as they tackle their tasks anew and prepare to move forward on their circuit one more time to a new community. Circus folks love the applause offered by those in the audience. It says, "You have been successful. You have touched us and moved us." It is an embrace of gratitude, an affirmation of the meaning of their efforts. It communicates, "We are with you. We feel the connection."

One example of the interconnectedness of audience and performers was given to me by the matriarch of a multi-generational circus family. When she was a young girl, the circus would end its run in each town by joining in the folk dance of that town. The practice may not be current in the United States but the attitude is still vibrant, we are in this together.

Preparing and presenting this exciting form of entertainment is the reason for every other aspect of the circus folk's lifestyle. The famed Karl Wallenda is quoted as saying, "Walking the wire is life. Everything else is just waiting."[116]

Circus folks work hard to create an illusion of reality in which all terrors and potential conflicts are resolved with happy endings. With great amazement, we watch very real dangers and challenges conquered with dazzling skill and style.[117]

---

116 Tino Wallenda. *Walking the Straight and Narrow: Lessons in Faith from the High Wire,* (Gainesville, FL: Bridge-Logos, 2005) 97.
117 Serious injuries in the circus are less common today than in the past. There are many strict safety procedures in force. But almost every circus person knows someone who has died or been severely injured in connection with a performance. One young woman remarked, "Backstage you think everything is magic but everything is dangerous."

In the circus world as in other forms of performance entertainment, the phrase, "The show must go on," is a powerful credo. Whenever possible, performers shrug off their pain and work through temporary disabilities. A clown suffering all the misery of the flu in the afternoon, weakly pausing as he walks toward his trailer, manages by the evening show to brandish a smile on entering the ring for his regular routine. Others with some rather serious muscle sprains and strains complete their acts with no hint of their distress. Another clown needing a doctor to drain fluid from a painfully swollen knee continued to accomplish his demanding climbs and dances show after show until the scheduled appointment date arrived. Some have even postponed surgery until the season has ended.

Those who witness accidents of even those dear to them, generally take their scheduled cue and continue to elicit joy and evoke wonder among those who have come to see the show, despite the personal suffering they are experiencing at the time.[118] In many cases there is no one who can step in and complete another person's routine. Like parents and other essential figures in life everywhere, when circus folks cannot be present, everyone else's life needs to be rearranged if things are to carry on.

However, in some cases there is no choice but to take the time to heal. One young woman expressed how an injury led to some spiritual reflection. "I fell off the chiffon two years ago and I wasn't close to God. For two months I had to stay on the train and realized I was far from God…. Now I don't want to be far. It was like God shaking you to wake you up to what you are doing."

With all its consistent demands, the circus world is still the chosen lifestyle of many. It is a vocation joyfully embraced by many who respond to the call of the traveling show. One performer explained some of the attraction of the circus. "There's a connection that we have to …step out of our world that we live in and into

---

118 Occasionally witnessing someone else's severe injuries can lead a person to quit performing or to take some time off before returning to the ring. Some seek counseling to help them deal with their pain. Most often, however, it seems that circus people seek solace in one another's company. In times of such distress, if the Sisters are in that circus they will arrange a prayer service for those who want to bring their concerns to God as a community. If there is a death, Father Jerry Hogan, national chaplain for the people of the circus, will find a way to be present to those who are grieving and will often celebrate Mass with them.

another world which represents magic and possibilities and joy, not always understanding that they're the same world." He followed his reflections by reciting this quotation from Henry Miller's "The Smile at the Foot of the Ladder,"

> The circus is a tiny closed off arena of forgetfulness. For a space it enables us to lose ourselves, to dissolve in wonder and bliss, to be transported by mystery. We come out of it in a daze, saddened and horrified by the everyday face of the world. But [it] is the only world and it is a world of magic, magic inexhaustible.[119]

In some domains a true artist can lose consciousness of self in the midst of a consuming performance. There is a moment of self-transcendence as one becomes the body-spirit accomplishing this feat, the motion is the person. The spiritual nature of this experience presents itself to the observer as dazzling grace. Some of those watching can themselves lose a sense of time and space and seem to enter into a communion of spirit with the actor before them.

In *The Mythic Imagination*, Stephen Larsen exclaims, "Everywhere in the circus we see fragments of the most ancient religion in the world still being celebrated; sacraments to the body which is capable of behaving like a spirit....The urge to see the body spiritualized, to fly, to break the tyranny of Newton's laws...is in our hollow bones."[120]

Throughout the show the circus has the aura of an order that is always verging on chaos. It goes to the edge and then, as one's breath alternates between gasps of fear and sighs of relief, it all ends safely and happily. Father Richard Notter, a priest of the Toledo Diocese, frequently ministers to circus people. He remarked that in competitive sports entertainment, the conclusion of the event is that one side wins and the other side loses. As a result some go home sad and some go home glad as they walk away from the arena. But at the circus, everybody wins and everyone can leave the show with a smiling face.[121]

---

[119] Henry Miller. *The Smile at the Foot of the Ladder*, (New York: New Directions Publishing Corporation, 1974. Original publication 1948) 48.

[120] Quoted in Sam Keen. *Learning to Fly: Trapeze – Reflections on Fear, Trust, and the Joy of Letting Go*, (New York: Broadway Books, 1999) 23.

[121] Father Richard Notter. Presentation at the 2008 Circus and Traveling Show Ministries Gathering in Florida. Father Notter is also the founder of the Catholic Migrant Farmworker Network.

Referring specifically to one dramatic act, Sam Keen describes this as an authentic spiritual aspect of circus life. "What is the gospel according to trapeze, its good news about the human condition? The artistry of the trapeze troupe emerges from a cooperative effort to create something of fleeting and fragile beauty. It knows danger but not violence, courage but not conquest, striving for excellence but not competition, the joy of achievement but not victory."[122]

As an ardent circus admirer, Keen also wrote, "The circus overwhelms us with improbable spectacles. It scrambles our categories. What is going on here? What kind of drama is being enacted in this theater of incarnate dreams? What kind of sacrament is being celebrated in this church of impossible possibilities?"[123]

Yet, this is not a fabricated illusion; it is a community of people stretching to the amazing limits of their native and highly developed abilities. As one woman told me, "In performance you make yourself the best in your area." Performers demonstrate the possibility of preparing well for the risks one takes to accomplish something significant. And all of this is done to lift the spirits of those who come to sit in the circle surrounding the center ring and to encourage them in their own journeys.

The audience provides the opportunity for circus folks to share their gifts and in that offering they encounter the divine center of life. Father David Tetrault names this as part of the "sacredness of play." According to a forty-five year old man, "The ability to bring happiness to people is much needed, especially children, this is our daily task. Working in the circus brings me closer to God every day." Another man, ten years older, remarked, "To me, joining the circus has introduced a spiritual life. What we do may be difficult, but in the end, it's your spiritual life."

A New York Times article quotes Tom Doherty, recognized as one of the most talented clowns of our day, saying, "Our job is to work in conspiracy with the audience to create joy."[124] The audience brings their life experiences and their expectations to the big top.

---

122 Sam Keen. *Learning to Fly: Trapeze – Reflections on Fear, Trust, and the Joy of Letting Go*, (New York: Broadway Books, 1999) 217.
123 Ibid., 24-25.
124 Harry Hurth, "Under the Big Top: Adopting a Persona with XXL Shoes," *The New York Times*, (March 22, 2008) C5.

The interaction is an important part of the whole circus experience for circus folks and audience alike. The more responsive the audience, the better the performances are. Despite their apparent bravado, those who put themselves out in front of an audience are taking a great psychic risk. One highly successful performer admitted, "I suffer from insecurity, fear of being discovered as an imposter. I think everyone has that fear inside somewhat."

A blasé group of spectators can put a damper on the spirits of circus workers as well as those in the audience with a brighter outlook. An expectant and appreciative crowd can heighten everyone's excitement. A veteran clown told me that, "As a first year clown, it is good to have an audience every day." The rhythm of performance is a give and take, a pattern of action and response.

Those circus folks who articulate their work from a consciously spiritual perspective envision the performance as a reflection of God, an invitation to wonder and awe that is not fulfilled unless it echoes in the heart of the audience. Their rapt attention and amazement are interpreted as an experience of the divine without words.

The performers enact feats of daring and delight which parallel the challenges and choices faced by everyone in their day-to-day lives. The analogies, consciously or unconsciously, resonate within the spirits of the spectators. As each daring feat is successfully completed and each humorous conundrum is adroitly resolved, men, women, and children of all ages, are released for a moment from their anxieties. Smiles and laughter express the relief which accompanies the freedom known in hope and joy.

The body is used to convey spiritual gifts. Offering the body in performance to lift others' spirits can be a prayer. To commit to doing this on a regular basis can be the response to a vocational call from God. Asked a survey question as to whether he used any particular religious practices to stay close to God, one performer said, "No religious practices. I consider what I do for a living God's work."

A reporter captured Sister Dorothy's response when asked about those who work in the circus: "'They're called by God to entertain, to bring joy to people's lives,' ...and that makes circus a sacred place. 'Take off your shoes,' she said, quoting Scripture, 'This is holy ground.'"

Some circus members consciously reflect on the spiritual metaphors that their unique lifestyle provides.

One experienced clown freely speaks about the spirituality of a clown. He suggests that the clown's routine of unwittingly walking into a difficulty which he cannot see but everyone else can, struggling through it with repeated failures, and then resolving the crisis, often with the encouragement of the audience, reflects a universal experience. God sees the source of our trials when they are unclear to us and points toward a way out, often with the support of wise and caring guides in our lives. The circus clown said, "We sacrifice our dignity to show others the way. We are crucifying ourselves on the cross of humor if you would."

New York Times journalist Harry Hurth had an opportunity to become a clown for one performance when Ringling Brothers Circus was in nearby East Rutherford, New Jersey. His reflections echo author Henry Miller's description of the four stages in such a performance: devotion, adoration, crucifixion, and resurrection. Hurth felt the devotion to the craft as he applied his makeup. The adoration followed as he interacted with members of the audience when he entered the ring in full costume. His crucifixion was not the loss of dignity inherent in so many clown routines, but rather the moment when he had to remove his face paint and return to his ordinary identity. However, his moment of resurrection ensued when he passed a little girl he had entertained earlier in his clown persona and, in a moment of recognition, she waved at him.[125]

Author Sam Keen reflects on the spiritual impact of watching the artists who make apparently effortless moves high above their audience. "The short leap from the trapeze to the catcher is a flight from primal fear to basic trust, from I to Thou, from autonomy to communion, that can only be made by a total commitment of the self. Flying, like faith, hope, and love, is an existential act that cannot be accomplished by a spectator."[126]

Whether consciously or unconsciously, circus people's commitment to provide a great performance for others provides

---

[125] Henry Hurth, "Under the Big Top: Adopting a Persona with XXL Shoes," *The New York Times*, (March 22, 2008) C5.

[126] Sam Keen. *Learning to Fly: Trapeze – Reflections on Fear, Trust, and the Joy of Letting Go*, (New York: Broadway Books, 1999) 56.

a spiritual resource for the audience as well. The very fact that they exist in a world of short-lived contracts, means that those who wish to perform must be open to constantly creating new possibilities. Life is never finished, settled, set in concrete. It is instead a growing, ever fresh garden with new blossoms set to open at any given time. The choreographers, creative directors, and production personnel take the varied offerings presented to them and design a new expression of mystery and delight for all who are willing to enter into their imaginative vision of life in the coming season.

Pope John Paul II reinforced the value of circus performance during the seventh International Congress of Circus and Fairground Artists: "Your profession, far from easy and certainly special, can be a privileged opportunity to proclaim authentic human values in the world's squares. In an age in which nothing seems to count but the frenzy of production and the accumulation of wealth, the gifts of joy and festivity are a real witness to those non-material values essential to a life of brotherhood and gratuitousness. You can set a unique example of a travelling Church that prays, listens, proclaims and cultivates brotherhood."[127]

A particular aspect of performance as a gift to others is found when the artists offer their talents to serve those in physical, emotional, or spiritual need.

Tino Wallenda, amazing tightrope walker, balances with ease on a chair positioned in the center of a wire. His audience a group of prisoners; his performance space, a jailhouse room; his message, God is love. Wallenda, who grew up on the road with circus experience on both his parents' sides going back almost two hundred years, now often does circus performances as a spiritual ministry.[128] His own faith and faithfulness is the root of his outreach to others. In his book, *Walking the Straight and Narrow: Lessons in Faith from the High Wire*, Wallenda mentions a tour in Canada which required several moves a week. On that circuit,

---

[127] Pope John Paul II. "Address to the Circus and Fairground Artists Taking Part in Their Seventh International Congress," *People on the Move*, (December 2005, No. 99 Supplement).

[128] For more than four years Wallenda worked full time in his small family circus called "Circus Maranatha" to spread a message of God's love and power in the United States, Mexico, Canada, and Puerto Rico. However, expenses outstripped income and he returned to regular circus performances as his mainstay. Now he uses his free time to bring the message of faith to others.

he and his wife, Olinka, called ahead to find a church his family could attend in each town the circus visited.[129]

The Kingdom Circus mentioned earlier performed for charity as well as for congregational sponsors. The owners "tried to pull students from all religions, races, and backgrounds" to model the peaceable Reign of God. They took advantage of their special opportunities for interacting with the children who attended their performances. "We would not try to convert anyone, but would show them by our actions and teamwork how lovely the "Kingdom' could be." In addition to the paying venues which supported the effort, they also offered shows in nursing homes, mental institutions, and maximum security prisons.

The contemporary UniverSoul Circus, employing a majority of African-American performers and reaching out to the black community does some outright outreach as well. Its distinctly spiritual tenor is clear. As just one spiritual example, certain performances include Gospel music sung by local Christian youth choirs, invited to join the show for a day.

Some of the bigger circuses invite their clowns to be involved in visits to pediatric wards as a part of their regular job in the large cities where they perform. One clown who visited children with cancer in a local hospital during his time with the Big Apple Circus carries vivid memories of those sacred times. What he recalls is immeasurably painful, deeply humbling, and yet indelibly comforting. Children who faced difficult treatments as well as debilitating health often revived when they saw the costumed clowns arrive. On one visit the hospital staff directed the circus visitors to the room of a boy who had just died. The mother had requested that the clowns come to say good-bye to her son because they were the only people who had been able to bring a joyful response from the child in his final days. Heartbreak and the sustaining grace of knowing that he had made a difference in this little one's life remain with that clown now as they did at that sad moment so long ago.

---

[129] Tino Wallenda. *Walking the Straight and Narrow: Lessons in Faith from the High Wire*, (Gainesville, FL: Bridge-Logos, 2005) 101.

Such acts of generosity occur from individual impulse as well as from the connections made on corporate levels. Sister Dorothy told me of one circus owner who kept an eye out for people who went away from the ticket window when they heard the price. With a compassionate heart he would go out and give them tickets so that the poor could enjoy the show alongside those able to afford the price of admission. For those in the circus world life is not just about making money. It is an ongoing process of inviting others to join them in making the world a happier place.

In the spiritual quest as well as in the circus, life is not a solidified accomplishment that one builds. None of the goals one seeks, God, the community of faith, truth, beauty, goodness, or love, are rooted primarily in a discrete place.

The search for these treasures is completed on the journey itself not at an elusive endpoint. And one of the tasks for the spiritual seeker is a successive series of attempts to blend one's gifts and talents into a meaningful whole.

One's performance in youth or at any other age, no matter how elegant, is not something one can frame, cling to, and admire. The living self grows and develops, sheds some strengths and attains new skills. Virtues are cultivated. Tendencies to make unloving choices are restrained. One makes new friends and loses other loved ones. There is a need to re-choreograph all that is changing into a grace-full presentation of the self in this season of life.

Choreographer God puts forward the design, the sacred show is prepared. The dance begins, performers take their places, and in the midst, missteps are transformed into new formations, true steps lead to grander combinations. Creator God responds, reshapes, anticipates, and reconfigures the living performance of grace in human hearts. Crooked lines are made straight; what look like failures become the prelude to glorious resurrections. The Divine Presence has not left us on our own; the Holy One watches our steps with immeasurable love. When the show has come to an end, the God of Love will join in the celebration. "Your God is in your midst….He will renew you by His love; he will dance with shouts of joy for you as on a day of festival." (Zephaniah 3:17)

CHAPTER 8

Concluding Remarks

"God sits enthroned above the circle of the earth.... God stretches out the heavens like a canopy, and spreads them out like a tent to live in." (Isaiah 40:22)

Two tall figures recede from the arena, moving toward the living quarters of the circus personnel. One is in full clown costume, among the seventh generation of performers in his family. The other is in jeans and a sports shirt. As they walk they talk about home and family and ordinary life. When they enter the entertainer's trailer home, his wife and little girl greet the men. In the compact space, the performer takes a seat near the tiny bathroom, the clown prepares to remove his makeup. Immediately his young daughter skips over, takes up a cloth and says, "I'll help you, daddy."

The charming scene, the rare privilege of sharing the intimate family moment with this great clown, is all a revelation to the newcomer. The acclaimed performer who has just brought hundreds of people to tears of laughter is an ordinary man. The child helps the parent to reveal himself, to remove the face he shows to the world, to make the transition from public figure to be himself at home.

The externals necessary to provide an entertaining show do not express who this person is in the context of his home life. Later the visitor finds out that this star reads Bible stories to his children and his wife holds a Bible study with other circus folk on a regular basis. Their faith in Jesus Christ is the center of their home.

The visitor's conversion was a transition from knowing the façade of the clown in his performance role to knowing the real person who created that performance persona and offers it as a work of joy and hope for others. The image of the little girl helping her clown dad take off his makeup is touching. She is revealing him as the person he is on a deeper, truer level, not just in the role he performs for others, although that is precious as well.

What is it like to go out every day and virtually become someone else; to perform for those who are counting on you to amaze, amuse, and enrich their lives with your particular skills and then to come home and make the transformation to mundane joys, cares, dreams, and relationships? Many people could ask the question about their own circumstances. It sounds like a description of most people's lives. In many ways it is.

An individual may not literally cover his/her skin with face paint or put on elaborate costumes but many people have a persona which is put on for work life and a dress code they adopt for their jobs. There are other variations of the clothing and face one presents to the world in other circumstances as well, different masks and uniforms for various occasions. Many people spend time trying to determine what is appropriate for each situation based largely on what others expect in that situation. We put on our game face. We don our party clothes to match the occasion.

Sometimes this process is disconcerting as an individual tries to blend his/her unique identity with what other people want. Discovering the inner life of circus folks may help some other folks to take off their own makeup and look at the self behind the performance they provide for the sake of their audience. Those who peer into the mirror of real circus life may get a better look at their own deeper, truer selves.

Many people have some type of deliberately applied psychic makeup on, often when they are performing roles for others. This can be a very good and important thing to do. Yet, it is important to know who is at the core of these various performative actions.

There is a coordinating center of one's being which orchestrates the features to be displayed in distinct settings. There is the character one is becoming through varied responses to relationships with customers, casual acquaintances, co-workers, and perhaps a larger public audience. Each person, of necessity, belongs to various groups. There is a need to fit in with appropriate behaviors for each situation. But above all there is a desire to center one's self. Even in the midst of running around in circles, in a type of three ring circus, where the lived experience feels like one of constant juggling, or keeping on track the many spinning plates of our various acts of love and service, the inner self wants to be steady and secure.

Some people face an apparent dissonance between their inner experience and the external demands made on them by acting differently at home and at work. Co-workers and neighbors may see one persona while the family knows someone very different.

For other people, balancing their own needs and the needs of others is perceived as too difficult. They attempt to restrict themselves to circumstances where their own comfort and preferences can be expressed without restraint.[130]

At times the lure of the circus is that it is seen as a chance to escape from the demands placed on us by everyone else in our lives. We want to run away to the circus. It seems so far from ordinary life, from a regular routine. The reality is, however, that we take ourselves with us wherever we go. And, although there is constant movement from place to place, the circus has its own continual routine, where one may repeat the same performance up to four-hundred times in a single season.

In circus life, breathtaking beauty and bravado fashioned from rigorous routine and persistent practice rotates each day with the ordinary rituals of family life and friendships which is the common lot of humankind. At every arrival in a new location, this roving band of entertainers is perceived by outsiders as aloof from the shared reality of local life in that town or city. Circus folks are a troupe of extraordinary folks passing through the space where ordinary life occurs for those in Main Town, USA.

---

[130] The hippie movement comes to mind. It rejected many societal expectations for clothing and behavior. Yet, it had its own strictures. It is doubtful if anyone would have been accepted in a commune if she or he preferred tailored slacks and blouses. And, on a practical level, adamant refusal to go anywhere where one is not accepted just as one is can gravely limit opportunities for full use of one's talents, employment, or extended social interactions.

At the same time, the traveling troupe's migrant lives revolve in a quite predictable pattern of its own. There is a circular route, an encircled performance, a sphere of circus companions on this journey through town after town. This is ordinary life to circus people and they in turn, can view the patterns of behavior among those in the cities they visit as unusual and somewhat unruly in comparison to the regular pattern which constitutes the rapid but repetitive cycle of circus life on the road.

The imaginary circus life one might envision has many elements of fantasy. The reality is that the circus is made up of talented and courageous people who perform in front of hundreds and sometimes thousands of people night after night. They go to their limits to delight and uplift the spirits of others who come to see them. But they have spirits also, sometimes joyful and sometimes downcast. Circus people need a deep connection to the spiritual life to sustain them in their outward-directed gift of themselves.

They know the regular death and resurrection pattern familiar to all human life. Particularly in Winter Quarters old acts are left behind to make way for new routines. The old show is gone and a new performance is being shaped. As a result some people have to leave. Some are chosen to remain on the show and some new members are invited to join the troupe. The whole community is reformulated and the task of becoming a living, loving unity starts all over again. What remains the same is the soul of each circus person, the individuals who seek to ground their lives and their relationships in a spiritual reality that does not change.

And since each person takes him/herself wherever he/she goes, leaving one's circumstances may not revolutionize one's heart. Rather than leaving one's home to join the circus, it may be beneficial to let circus wisdom be a lens through which to view everyday life. Before one starts traveling away from ordinary life, running away to the circus, there are some questions to consider. Looking at one's self in the here and now, how would we characterize our spiritual center. Who am I in the home of my inner self? What roots me in the reality of my existence within God? Where is my sacred space on the journey of life? What do interdependence and ministry mean in the unique constellation of my relationships? How can my routine performance be part of the divine "conspiracy to create joy?"

Pursuing answers to these questions can be part of clarifying one's spiritual path and developing a life more deeply centered in God. The evolving spiritual person advances toward handling the dilemmas of life with serenity and integrity and expressing an inner true self in the most varying circumstances with all their distinct demands. In the process of bringing forth appropriate responses from inner resources, the growing spiritual person develops ways to be true to self while genuinely serving others' needs. These are marks of circus spirituality.

The spiritual life of the circus world is firmly founded on communal interdependence. Knowing and accepting the true self as a person enmeshed in community, the maturing spiritual agent realizes the interconnectedness of all life. Dedicating self to enhancing all that exists in life inspires self-enrichment and full expression of the individual's own being and potential abilities. The loner is not the ideal. Even the hermit, to be holy, must take the community along into the desert. Otherwise the life of solitude results in an arid soul to match the barren environment. In any case, few are called to that life apart. Most people are called to the life in common, in the midst of the crowd.

Circus spirituality is far from a solitary spirituality. It is a life lived in the presence of many in audiences far and wide. At the same time it is a life lived in intimacy with other circus folks who are uniquely bound to one another. Within its special constellation of movement, performance schedules, and closely arranged living quarters, the spirituality of circus life is an everyday spirituality. It is formed in the rhythm of daily life where prayer, and love, and grace flow out and in. It is a spirituality of *lo cotidiano*.[131] Ana Maria Pineda describes this as "the concept of the ordinary as the locus of the sacred. *Lo cotidiano* is a spirituality where the ordinary is experienced as the locus of the sacred."[132]

In a 2004 article in *Theological Studies*, Pineda reflects on this experience in Latino/a life where "everyday activities of life open themselves to the sacred and to the need for God in one's ordinary

---

[131] This phrase has been used by Ada Maria Isasi Diaz, Orlando Espin, and Maria Pilar Aquino among others to describe a spirituality rooted in everyday reality.

[132] Ana Maria Pineda. "Imagenes de Dios en el Camino: Retablos, Ex-Votos, Milagritos, and Murals," *Theological Studies*. (Washington, June 2004, Vol. 65, Iss. 2) 368.

life."[133] This makes everyday spirituality/*lo cotidiano* a realistic model which many can embrace no matter how hectic and stressful their schedule nor how closely they are being scrutinized. This is the stuff of life, to find a way to live a deep spiritual life in the midst of a materially demanding reality. It embraces the stance taken by spiritually alive members of the circus community.

A thirty-year old woman explained, "Every time I work, if I am in pain, I say, 'This is for you. I offer this to you.' The circus life is really hard and if you don't have faith, you don't have belief that God will get you to the next town.... Everyday is something...This is our life. We just try to live it the way God teaches us."

Reflecting on possible challenges to spiritual life in life on the road, one circus-ministry Sister had this to say:

> I don't think it is difficult if you feel at home with the rhythm and lifestyle. Except it's a rhythm that is very tiring. Tiredness can definitely affect one's spiritual life. (Perhaps not always negatively, though; it depends on how I manage that tiredness.) The risks of being on the road can 'feed' our spiritual life, if we let them, as can the closeness to nature, working outdoors so much of the time, as well as the closeness to one another...as well as the sense of community and of a common project. Even the fact of eating together in a common cookhouse can 'feed' my spiritual life, too.

In trying to understand circus spirituality, there are some published studies which may shed light on the type of spiritual approach taken by those in this special subgroup of migrant workers. Social circumstances seem to affect spiritual meaning as much as other aspects of life. Susan Sullivan, in her article, "The Work-Faith Connection for Low-Income Mothers," makes the point that for the economically challenged women in her study "the primary role (of faith) is not to contribute meaning but rather to aid in surviving the low-wage service sector."[134]

The main role religious faith played in the lives of the low-income respondents was to help them with work-related stress.

---
133 Ibid.
134 Susan Crawford Sullivan. "The Work-Faith Connection for Low-Income Mothers: A Research Note," *Sociology of Religion*, (Washington: Spring 2006, Vol. 67, Iss. 1) 99.

Another strong effect described was in helping them with job performance. Additional connections between work and faith included workplace ethics and helping them to find work. Some attitudes similar to those to Sullivan's respondents are reflected in the circus survey responses. Circus workers are generally not high-income earners.

These results vary from than those obtained by Robert Wuthnow whose research focused on workers earning at a higher income level. The analysis indicated that for those who are financially comfortable, the main way in which faith affects work is by providing greater motivation for doing one's particular job. A belief system helps the person of faith to understand that there is a spiritual meaning in doing one's work. The individual sees him/herself as contributing to the greater good, participating in God's continuing creation, and/or using fully the gifts received from the creator. Reviewing the results of his study, Wuthnow concludes, "… that religious commitment has come to play a kind of therapeutic role in relation to economic behavior in postindustrial society… Rather than providing guidance, religious conviction contributes meaning-that is, work becomes more interesting… because it has cosmic significance."[135] Here, too, there are similarities between the results of the circus respondents and those of Wuthnow's study.

The circus worker is frequently a low-wage earner, with no benefits unless employed by one of the largest circuses. So, the impact of faith might tend toward the type of effect related by Sullivan for low-income workers. And, in fact, the circus respondents often mention that they frequently offer prayers of petition for help in dealing with the difficulties of their work life. Some also indicated a conviction that God assisted them in getting their present job. Performers, in particular, mention praying that they do their routines well. A distinction is that many non-performers also pray for the performers' success.

On the other hand, circus employment is generally a voluntarily chosen lifestyle as well, and has its own status for those who value circus life. The high regard people have for the value of circus entertainment might cause the influence of religious belief to affect them in some ways more akin to those in Wuthnow's study,

---

[135] Robert Wuthnow. *God and Mammon in America*, (New York: The Free Press, 1994) 77.

those whose high status is determined by the size of their paycheck and corporate position. And indeed, the survey results indicate that a number of circus workers experience their work as holy. They are aware of a sacred nature in their work. They describe their purpose in circus work as sharing in God's creative activity, providing the audience a time of relief from the burdens of life, and enhancing the joy and beauty of life.

A recent event underlines this approach. A group of circus folks joined me in giving a presentation at the College of St. Elizabeth in Morristown, New Jersey. When a member of the audience asked whether their lives in the circus were truly as spiritual as my descriptions had implied, the circus folks eagerly vied with one another to answer the question. Each one strongly asserted that the experience of circus was the most spiritual life they had known. One of the speakers, veteran clown Tom Doherty, responded to a follow-up question on why people choose lower paying jobs in the circus over making more money using the college degrees he and a good number of other circus folks have earned. His quick and confident reply was, "There are other types of currency than money."

So the criteria of the two studies mentioned above both concur in some way with the circumstances of circus people. They generally do not have high wages but they often do consider themselves to be rather fortunate. They see themselves as part of a noble endeavor which enriches the humanity of all those for whom they present their ritual celebrations of grace, surprise, power, and joy.

The distinct results of each research project correspond in some way to circus spirituality. On the one hand faith offers a sense of purpose for those who see themselves as blessed to be part of the great circus tradition. On the other hand, the lack of security in finances and other risky aspects of circus life focus a significant amount of the circus traveler's daily prayer toward survival. One man seems to blend both approaches in his beliefs: "Being in the circus keeps me connected to God. I constantly thank Him for allowing me to be a magician and circus performer. Only people who don't *love* their jobs want to retire from them. I hope I never have to retire from the circus. The constant travel and the hazards of travel and the type of work we do keeps my focus on my Heavenly Father."

Concluding Remarks

The prayer of the spiritual circus person is the prayer of the dependent ones – of those "on the Edge" – the poor, the stressed, those in danger. One woman mentioned her understanding that others outside the circus world have their own problems that, though different, call for the same confidence in God. "You pray for more strength. Here there is more need to pray for help. Other places, people have more bills. They have it difficult in other ways....God squeezes you but not too hard. He helps you little by little. He is there though you don't see him."

In the circus survey, the most frequently mentioned prayers were prayers of thanks and prayers for help, especially for protection of the performers during the show. The very hazards they encounter seem to underscore the presence of God. Circus people pray for one another and for themselves. One woman said, "I always prayed before I went up to the trapeze for God to watch over and protect us all. I give thanks at the end of the day for the day." A thirty-year old who performs while hanging by her long and beautiful hair from the heights of the tent said, "Whenever I go up high, I think of Him and pray." A thirty-one year old woman exclaimed, "Everybody I know of prays before you go in the ring and also before a trip, at least I did!" And a mother talked about calling on God when her children go into the tent to perform, "Parents always have God's name on their lips."

Some of the expressed effects of such pre-performance prayer were described as a sense of calm, of well-being, and of security. A seventy-six year old man was convinced that, "More than ninety percent of the artists commend themselves to God before each act."

In his 2005 book, famed tight-rope walker, Tino Wallenda, remarks, "…working in a job that puts your life on the line everyday tends to keep you in the present moment, and ingrains in you a spirit of gratitude and celebration."[136]

A priest who has spent time working in the circus said, "No suburbia masks endure here. People must confront who they are. Also the danger, and being separated from family and the resulting loneliness helps people turn to God." Homesickness

---

[136] Tino Wallenda. *Walking the Straight and Narrow: Lessons in Faith from the High Wire*, (Gainesville, FL: Bridge-Logos, 2005) 122.

and the isolation of those who do not easily learn the languages of those around them are frequent challenges. Some overcome these obstacles quickly, others take longer.

An interesting statistic in the circus survey is that while fifty-seven percent of the respondents indicated that there are aspects of circus life that make it difficult to live a spiritual life and stay close to God, eighty-eight percent said that there are things about circus life that help them to live a spiritual life and stay close to God.

Among the aspects of circus life credited with helping circus people to stay close to God and live a spiritual life, survey respondents named the difficulties of the life, seeing nature, living so close to others, and having a close family life, along with many other reasons. One woman said it helps that many circus people have their "roots in love of family and God."

A sixty-four year old woman spoke about sustaining a spiritual life in the circus, "It is all around you every day." A young woman, when asked what helps her stay close to God in the circus, replied, "The hard life. It helps you because you need more. When everything is good, maybe you forget God. You don't need him or just relax." An older woman remarked on how circus keeps her close to God, "Because everything changes everyday, I think the immediacy keeps God fresh in your mind."

Looking at the lives and spiritual realities of Mexican immigrants in his book, *Border of Death, Valley of Hope*, Daniel Groody asks two key questions spirituality. How does migration shape people's understanding of a relationship to God? What have religious communities done to respond to migrants' special needs? The reflections in these pages have directed similar questions to a nomadic group of companions whose journeys are ongoing. The path they traverse is not towards a specific geographical endpoint. They are more of a traveling tribe, following a winding trail for a purpose other than arrival. One circus troupe member described the circus collective as "a small community of diverse cultures [who] live together and respect each other."

In line with Groody's questions, the wanderings of circus folks do shape their spiritual lives. They do this by keeping them in close communion with one another in a way that separates them from

Concluding Remarks

the communities through whom they travel. Their interdependence urges them toward mutual respect and care. Fragility in the face of danger and the tenuous nature of their employment both direct them toward dependence on the Divine. The need to carry their possessions from place to place dictates simplicity and detachment.

And what have religious communities done to respond to their special needs? Well, the women religious whose efforts have been outlined throughout this work bring the care of the faith community to the migrant circus workers. The priests who sustain an ongoing relationship with these traveling entertainers provide links to the broader church community and sacramental sustenance. The circus members who already serve as catechists and those in formation for that ministry, are offering service leadership in imitation of Christ. The clergy who respond to the circus visitors in their midst and offer pastoral ministry when the circus comes to town affirm the value of each person to the community of faith in that local setting. The members of convents who offer hospitality to the Missionary Sisters and the Little Sisters on their journeys, support those who serve and refresh them for continued ministry. But there is so much more that could be done.

A 2003 Gallup study indicates that sixty percent of American adults say that faith is involved in every aspect of their lives; seventy percent feel a need to experience spiritual growth in their daily lives, and seventy percent find purpose and meaning in life because of their religious faith.[137] While the exact questions used by Gallup were not repeated in the circus survey, the results of the circus study strongly support the conclusion that circus people in the United States parallel the Gallup respondents in terms of the importance of faith in everyday life and the desire for spiritual growth.[138] There is a clear impression that for many in the circus their faith provides the essential source of purpose and meaning in their lives.[139]

---

137 Retrieved from www.gallup.com.
138 Evidence of spirituality is not limited to United States' circuses. After the death of a acrobat in a Mexican circus performing in the United States, a newspaper reporter cited other performers describing the victim as "a quiet man who was a devout Catholic and regularly prayed to La Virgen de Dan Juan de Los Lagos..." Los Angeles Times, (May 1, 2007).
139 The 30% for whom faith is not uppermost in their lives in the Gallup survey have their parallels in the circus. One young Russian woman said, "I don't believe in God. ...My mother believes. When I was a child...I had a ceremony with the cross. She told me I am Christian Orthodox. I have tried to talk to God one time. It was easy, not difficult."

The circus spirituality of intimate and personal relationship to God in the details of life resonates with that of many holy people including Therese of Lisieux and Ignatius of Loyola. It is the practice of the presence of God associated with Brother Lawrence for whom:

> "The time of action does not differ from the time of prayer. I possess God as peacefully in the bustle of my kitchen, where sometimes several people are asking me for different things at the same time, as I do upon my knees before the Blessed Sacrament" and who referred to maintaining communion with God's presence by saying, "There is nothing complicated about it. One has only to turn to it honestly and simply.[140]

Communion with God in the circus world conforms to spiritualities which understand that God speaks to individuals in the circumstances of their lives; that life is experienced in God's presence always, and that the hardship of missionary life in its attempts to bring the good news far and wide can keep one close to God because one is so dependent on power beyond oneself. For theologian and author Virgilio Elizondo this is where the ordinary and divine come together, a unity created in the "little stories" of people's lives. It is a truly incarnational spirituality.

The simplicity of Bethlehem's surroundings for the most profound coming of God into human reality is mirrored in circus life. Many of the interviews referenced in this book took place on folding chairs. A lumbering elephant grazed in the background of one conversation disdaining any interest in what was being said. In another interview, a curious zedonk (half zebra, half donkey) poked a considerable nose between the caretaker and myself as we talked.

Outside a trailer's entryway, under the tented Big Top, or in the Ladies' Wardrobe, the ubiquitous folding chair highlighted the impermanence of every site and the flexibility of each person with whom I came in contact. Many interviews took place in between shows. Several were completed in two parts, interrupted midstream by a performer's dash to the center ring to entertain a waiting audience.

---

140 Brother Lawrence. *Practice of the Presence of God*, (Peabody, MA: Hendrickson Publishers, 2004).

Concluding Remarks

It is with great gratitude that I recall the circus folks who shared some of their precious time to contribute to these reflections. They generously wrote down their thoughts in their native English, Spanish, or Portuguese, or gave them orally in English, either as their first language or with overtones of their homes in Russia, France, or one of several Spanish-speaking countries. Remarkably open, most were eager to talk about God and their relationship with God whom they typically envision as parent, creator, or friend. Even those who began to participate with some reticence gradually responded quite freely and with evident sincerity. My admiration of their various talents and physical fortitude expanded into a deep appreciation of the spiritual strength and inner grace they possess and project in their everyday lives.

The good news that circus folks bring with them is in the performance. It provides the motivating force for the mixture of backstage workers and entertainers from diverse countries and backgrounds to form a single community. The performance is their gift to the broader world. It provides a metaphor for many aspects of life. The spiritual meaning of the acts can enrich and sustain the spiritual perspective of circus people as well as members of the audience. It echoes the earlier quotation from the performer who calls this reality a "conspiracy to create joy" with the audience.

One of the survey respondents described an example of this phenomenon:

> You have the trapeze artist standing on the platform, the drum rolls low, the Ringmaster announces the triple somersault, a legendary trick. The audience has a hush. Why? Because this guy's about to throw a triple somersault in mid-air and maybe, or maybe not, get caught. It's that risk. It's that leap into the unknown that he is demonstrating for us – but we all have to do that in our own lives. There has to be a degree of trust in that moment….All we notice is that leap into the air and for a moment he is suspended in hope that he'll catch, and that's why when he does catch, there's an Oh. It's a nice big response, or better yet, when they miss it and try it again and get it, there's always a huge response of relief and connection.

The dramatic aspects of life are concentrated in such intense moments of suspense in the circus, but other acts reflect different dimensions of life. A clown spoke of his role.

> "To me, circus represents life, if you will. Then the clown is a natural role in it because he delivers balance. He is the humor, the whimsical part of life." The clown is a marginal figure, someone very different than those who have come as spectators and even than the other performers. Interacting with those present without embarrassment at being so different, clowns "disregard worldly status and attributions.... The soul of the clown is loneliness.[141]

Those who have experienced the aloneness of being different from those around them, identify with the clown. While one laughs sympathetically with the clown's bumbling attempts at success, one can experience the pain of the clown's failure; rejoice in the clown's success. Those who have been on the outside of a group recognize themselves as the clown in many of life's performances. And the clown reciprocates the sharing of emotions, "The clown laughs as we do, and yet at the very best the clown cries, as we do."[142]

Yet, it is not just the entertaining circus performances which can provide metaphors for one's life. In a different vein, a view of the everyday life of those who make the circus happen can provide a revealing perspective on non-circus lives as well. What circus folks do everyday gives them a way to know and identify who God is. Reflecting on the stories they have shared, others can experience a sense of companionship with those in the circus. In doing so one may more readily identify the reality of God in one's own daily circumstances. It is possible to realize in a fresh way that no-one stands alone but that people who desire a life of faith belong to a communion of spiritual survivors, those who want to respond to God's care; to share God's love wherever life's journey takes us, whatever the challenges at hand.

---

141 Joas Adiprasetva. "Following Jesus the Clown: Jesus, Clown, and the Voice of Otherness," paper of a student at Boston University School of Theology, p. 6. Retrieved online at http://people.bu.edu/joas/tt871-jesusandclown.pdf on June 25, 2009.
142 Hugh Lewin, ed. *A Community of Clowns: Testimonies of People in Urban Rural Mission*, (Geneva: WCC Publication, 1987) 9.

Concluding Remarks

All of the allusions being made to the migrant circus workers' connection to the holy through a search for the sacred in space and time and community are an opening to the comparisons that can be made for that same search outside of circus life. Like so many other people those in the circus world value the transcendent and honor what is holy. Their spiritual life is a part of their everyday life. God is on the journey with the circus folks not merely when they have a brief respite in their winter quarters. God is there not only when they can attend community worship services but God is with them in every new stage of their circuit following the sun from Spring into Winter. God accompanies the community at the bright fresh start of a new season and stays through to the travel-weary finish when all eagerly await their seasonal break. And God is with every person outside of the circus in the same way, in the often fast, challenging, frequently repetitive circuit of every person's daily activities, from sun-up to sundown, day by day and year by year. The God of loving, creative grace and power is within and among and beyond all who journey. At every step along the path God is present, surrounding each precious person with unwavering care.

While it may be relatively easy to connect the image of God as the itinerant Jesus, on the move throughout his ministry, to the nomadic circus folks, there are many other rich connections. Those who reflect on circus spirituality may imagine new metaphors of God and God's relationship to all who are on the road. All descriptions of God are limited to the language of analogy. God is like a farmer. God is like an employer. God is like a parent. The gallery of images is limitless as is the Source of All That Is, the One who seekers attempt to characterize more clearly in each new age. With circus life in mind some novel illustrations may be discovered, creative ways to reveal hidden dimensions of the unfathomable God, the Holy One so present in daily lives lived in God's presence.

God is like the organizer of a three-ring circus, whose design includes the orchestration of all that exists into a harmonious creation, a culmination of all that God created as good and very good. And, as Nouwen has written, God is like the catcher in a trapeze act who calls us to leap into the emptiness with abandonment. God is like a clown, who empties self, becomes identified with the weak of this world, and is willing to be laughed at, in order to reveal for us the source of joy and hope, and save us from our sorrow.[143]

Spirituality may be described as one's pattern of responses to the action of the Spirit in one's everyday life. Those responses come from one's personal nature and history and are influenced by the circumstances in which one lives. And those responses themselves are prompted by the Holy Spirit.

One of the Little Sisters who has ministered for years in the circus assessed some of the deep graces of circus life. "In the circus… there is a 'world of symbolism' that can also feed our spiritual life: the sense of pilgrimage and journey, the new start we have each day with changing towns, the human and animal kingdom living in peace together…the present moment, the renouncements and letting go needed to create something beautiful…. There is also the Gospel call to bring joy to others."

These pages wind down simply with some highlights of the implications their content may have for everyday spirituality outside the circus. The key features of circus spirituality include the experience that any space can become sacred by intention. God is with us on the journey, in the midst of our ordinary lives wherever they take us. Love is expressed in mutual ministry. Awareness of a central purpose in life and knowing its meaning for others can keep spiritual people going forward in what really matters in life no matter what the challenges of their daily lives.

This parable of circus life is at an end. The story concludes with a circus blessing for all who have reflected on its message. The phrase below is the sincere good wish circus folks most commonly offer to others. With a conviction of the beauty and value of their very special way of life, it is my wish for you as well.

May all your days be circus days.

---

[143] The clown image has been applied frequently to Jesus. According to Harvey Cox, "Only by learning to laugh at the hopelessness around us can we touch the hem of hope. Christ the clown signifies our playful appreciation of the past and our comic refusal to accept the spectre of inevitability in the future. He is the incarnation of festivity and fantasy." Harvey Cox. *The Feast of Fools: A Theological Essay on Festivity and Fantasy*, (Cambridge: Harvard University Press, 1969) 142.